# HARRIET MARTINEAU.

# HARRIET MARTINEAU

BY

## MRS. F. FENWICK MILLER

KENNIKAT PRESS
Port Washington, N. Y./London

HARRIET MARTINEAU

First published in 1884
Reissued in 1972 by Kennikat Press
Library of Congress Catalog Card No: 70-160772
ISBN 0-8046-1604-3

Manufactured by Taylor Publishing Company    Dallas, Texas

# PREFACE.

THE material for this biographical and critical sketch
of Harriet Martineau and her works has been drawn
from a variety of sources. Some of it is quite new.
Her own *Autobiography* was completed in 1855 ; and
there has not hitherto been anything at all worth
calling a record of the twenty-one years during which
she lived and worked after that date. Even as regards
the earlier period, although, of course, I have drawn
largely for facts upon the *Autobiography*, yet I have
found much that is new to relate. For some information and hints about this period I am indebted to
her relatives, of her own generation, Dr. James Martineau, and Mrs. Henry Turner, of Nottingham, as
well as to one or two others. With reference to the
latest twenty-one years of her life, my record is entirely
fresh, though necessarily brief. Mrs. Chapman, of

Boston, U.S., has written a volume in completion of the *Autobiography*, which should have covered this later period; but her account is little more than a repetition, in a peculiar style, of the story that Miss Martineau herself had told, and leaves the later work of the life without systematic record. As a well-known critic remarked in *Macmillan*—" This volume is one more illustration of the folly of intrusting the composition of biography to persons who have only the wholly irrelevant claim of intimate friendship." But it should be remembered that when Miss Martineau committed to Mrs. Chapman the task of writing a memorial sketch, and when the latter accepted the undertaking, both of them believed that the life and work of the subject of it were practically over. I have reason to know that if Harriet Martineau had supposed it to be even remotely possible that so much of her life remained to be spent and recorded, she would have chosen someone more skilled in literature, and more closely acquainted with English literary and political affairs, to complete her " Life." Having once asked Mrs. Chapman to fulfil the task, however, Harriet Martineau was too loyal and generous a friend to remove it from her charge; and Mrs. Chapman, on her side, while continually begging instructions from her subject as to what she was to say, and while doubtless aware that she would not be adequate to the undertaking which had grown so since she accepted it, yet would not throw it off her hands. But her volume is in no degree a record of those last years, which constitute nearly a third of Harriet Martineau's whole life. I have had to seek facts and impressions about that period almost entirely from other sources.

My deepest obligations are due, and must be first expressed, to Mr. Henry G. Atkinson, the dearest friend of Harriet Martineau's maturity. It is commonly known that she forbade, by her will, the publication of her private letters; but she showed her supreme faith in and value for her friend, Mr. Atkinson, by specially exempting him from such prohibition. Her objection to the publication of letters was made on general grounds. Her own letters are singularly beautiful specimens of their class; and she declared that she would not mind if every word that ever she wrote were published; but she looked upon it as a duty to uphold the principle that letters should be held sacred confidences, just as all honourable people hold private conversations, not to be published without leave. But in authorising Mr. Atkinson to print her letters, if he pleased, she maintained that she was not departing from this principle; for it was only the same as it would be if two friends agreed to make their conversation known. I feel deeply grateful to Mr. Atkinson for allowing me the privilege of presenting some of her letters to the public in this volume, and of perusing very many more.

I have been permitted, also, to read a vast number of Harriet Martineau's letters addressed to other friends besides Mr. Atkinson, and how much they have aided me in following her work and in appreciating her personality, may easily be guessed; but, of course, I may not publish these letters. Amongst many persons to whom I am indebted for helping me to "get touch" with my subject in this way, I must specially thank two. Mr. Henry Reeve, the editor of the *Edinburgh Review*, was a relative and intimate friend of Harriet Martineau; and her correspondence with so distinguished a man of letters was, naturally, peculiarly interesting—not the less so because they differed altogether on many matters of opinion. Her letters, which Mr. Reeve has kindly allowed me to see, have been of very great service to me. Miss F. Arnold, of Fox How, (the youngest daughter of Dr. Arnold, of Rugby,) is the second to whom like particular acknowledgment is due. She was young enough to have been Harriet Martineau's daughter; but she was also a beloved friend, and was almost a daily visitor at "The Knoll" during the later years of Miss Martineau's life. The letters which Miss Arnold, during occasional absences from home, received from her old friend, are very domestic, lively, and characteristic of the writer. It has been of great value to me to have seen all the letters that have been lent me, but especially these two sets, so different and yet so similar as I have found them to be.

I have visited Norwich, and seen the house where Harriet Martineau was born ; Tynemouth, where she lay ill; Ambleside, where she lived so long and died at last ; and Birmingham, to see my valued friends, her nieces and nephew. If I should thank by name all with whom I have talked of her, and from whom I have learned something about her, the list would grow over-long ; and so I must content myself with thus comprehensively expressing my sense of individual obligations to all who have laid even a small stone to this little memorial cairn.

F. F. M.

# CONTENTS.

———

# HARRIET MARTINEAU.

## CHAPTER I.

### THE CHILD AT HOME AND AT SCHOOL.

WHEN Louis XIV. of France revoked the Edict of
Nantes, in 1688, a large number of the Protestants who
were driven out of France by the impending persecu-
tions came to seek refuge in this favoured land of
liberty of ours. Many who thus settled in our midst
were amongst the most skilful and industrious workers,
of various grades, that could have been found in the
dominions of the persecuting king who drove them
forth. They must have been, too, in the nature of
the case, strong-hearted, clear in the comprehension
of their principles, and truthful and conscientious
about matters of opinion ; for the cowardly, the weak,
and the false could stay in their own land. From the
good stock of these exiles for conscience-sake sprang
Harriet Martineau.

Her paternal Huguenot ancestor was a surgeon, who
was married to a fellow-countrywoman and co-reli-

gionist of the name of Pierre. This couple of exiles
for freedom of opinion settled in Norwich, where the
husband pursued his profession. Their descendants
supplied a constant succession of highly-respected
surgeons to the same town, without intermission, until
the early part of this century, when the line of
medical practitioners was closed by the death of Harriet
Martineau's elder brother at less than thirty years old.
The Martineau family thus long occupied a good professional position in the town of Norwich.

Harriet's father, however, was not a surgeon, but a
manufacturer of stuffs, the very names of which are
now strange in our ears—bombazines and camlets.
His wife was Elizabeth Rankin, the daughter of a
sugar-refiner of Newcastle-on-Tyne. A true North-
umbrian woman was Mrs. Martineau; with a strong
sense of duty, but little warmth of temperament; with
the faults of an imperious disposition, and its correla-
tive virtues of self-reliance and strength of will. These
qualities become abundantly apparent in her in the
story of her relationship with her famous daughter.
On both sides, therefore, Harriet Martineau was endowed by hereditary descent with the strong qualities
—the power, the clear-headedness, and the keen conscience—which she interfused into all the work of
her life.

Thomas and Elizabeth Martineau, her father and
mother, were the parents of eight children, two of
whom became widely known and influential as thinkers
and writers. Harriet was the sixth of the family, and
was born at Norwich, in Magdalen Street, on the 12th
of June, 1802, the mother being at that time thirty
years old. The next child, born in 1805, was the boy
who grew up to become known as Dr. James Mar-

tineau; so that the two who were to make the family
name famous were next to each other in age. Another
child followed in this family group, but not until 1811,
when Harriet was nine years old, so that she could
experience with reference to this baby some of that
tender protective affection which is such an education
for elder children, and so delightful to girls with
strong maternal instincts such as she possessed.

The sixth child in a family of eight is likely to
be a personage of but small consequence. The parents'
pride has been somewhat satiated by previous experiences of the wonders of the dawning faculties of their
children; and the indulgence which seems naturally
given to "the baby" gets comparatively soon trans-
ferred from poor number six to that interloper number
seven. Mrs. Martineau, too, was one of that sort of
women who, as they would say, do not "spoil" their
children. Ready to work for them, to endure for them,
to struggle to provide them with all necessary comforts, and even with pleasures, at the cost, if need be,
of personal sacrifice of comfort and pleasure, such
mothers yet do not give to their children that bountiful
outpouring of tender, caressing, maternal love, which
the young as much require for their due and free
growth as plants do the flood of the summer sunshine.
To starve the emotions in a child is not less cruel than
to stint its body of food. To repress and chain up the
feelings is to impose as great a hardship as it would be
to fetter the freedom of the limbs. Mothers who have
laboured and suffered through long years for the
welfare of their children, are often grieved and pained
in after days to find themselves regarded with respect
rather than with fondness; but it was they themselves
who put the seal upon the fountains of affection at the

time when they might have been opened freely—and whose fault is it if, later, the outflow is found to be checked for evermore?

The pity of it is that such mischief is often wrought by parents who love their children intensely, but who err in the management of them for want of the wisdom of the heart, the power of sympathetic feeling, which is seen so much stronger sometimes in comparatively shallow natures than in the deeper ones that have really more of love and of self-sacrifice in their souls. Those who lack tenderness either of manner or feeling, those to whom the full and free expression of affection is difficult or seems a folly, may perhaps be led to reflect, by the story of Harriet Martineau's childhood, on the suffering and error that may result from a neglect of the moral command: "Parents, provoke not your children to wrath."

"My life has had no spring," wrote Harriet Martineau, sadly; yet there was nothing in the outer circumstances of her childhood and youth to justify this feeling. Her mother's temper and character were largely responsible for what Harriet calls her "habit of misery" during childhood. It is right to explain, however, that this unhappiness was doubtless partly due to physical causes. She was a weakly child, her health having been undermined by the dishonesty of the wet nurse employed for her during the first three months of her life. The woman lost her milk, and managed to conceal the fact until the baby was found to be in an almost dying condition from the consequences of want of nourishment. How far her frequent ill-health, during many succeeding years, was to be ascribed to this cannot be known; but her mother naturally attributed all Harriet's delicacy of health to this cause, even the deafness from which she suffered, although this did not become pronounced till she was over twelve years of age.

Her deafness, which was the most commonly known of her deficiencies of sensation, was not her earliest deprivation of a sense. She was never able to smell, that she could remember; and, as smell and taste are intimately joined together, and a large part of what we believe to be flavour is really odour, it naturally followed that she was also nearly destitute of the sense of taste. Thus two of the avenues by which the mind receives impressions from the outer world were closed to her all her life, and a third was also stopped before she reached womanhood. The senses are the gates by which pleasure as well as pain enter into the citadel where consciousness resides. Of all the senses, those which most frequently give entrance to pleasure, and seldomest to pain, were those which she had lost. "When three senses out of five are deficient," as she said, "the difficulty of cheerful living is great, and the terms of life are truly hard."

She suffered greatly, even as a little child, from indigestion. Milk, in particular, disagreed with her; but it was held essential by Mrs. Martineau that children should eat bread and milk, and for years poor Harriet endured daily a lump at her chest and an oppression of the spirits, induced by her inability to digest her breakfast and supper. Nightmares, and causeless apprehensions in the day, also afflicted the nervous and sensitive girl, and she had "hardly any respite from terror."

A child so delicate in health could not have been very happy under any home conditions. Only a truly wise and tender maternal guardianship could have

made the life of such an one at all tolerable; but
Harriet Martineau was one of the large family of a
sharp-tempered, masterful, stern, though devoted
mother, whose cleverness found vent in incessant sar-
casm, and in whom the love of power natural to a
capable, determined person degenerated, as it so often
does in domestic life, into a severe despotism.

Mrs. Martineau's circumstances were such as to
increase her natural tendency to stern and decided
rule.   Dr. Martineau tells me that all who knew his
mother feel that Harriet does not do justice in her
" Autobiography " to that mother's nobler qualities,
both moral and intellectual, and especially the latter.
Harriet and James Martineau, like so many other men
and women of mark, were the children of a mother of
uncommon mental capacity.   Her business faculties
were so good, and her judgment so clear, that her
husband (a man of a sweet and gentle disposition)
invariably took counsel with her about all his affairs,
and acted by her advice.   There are still inhabitants
of Norwich who remember Mrs. Martineau, and their
testimony of her is identical with her son's.   " She
was the ruling spirit in that house," says one of them.
" Whatever was done there, you understood that it
was she who did it."   The way in which this gentleman came to know so much of her corroborates Dr.
Martineau's declaration that " she was really devoted
to her children, and would do anything for them; if
we were miserable in our childhood [a fact which
he does not dispute] it could not be said to be consciously her fault."   Mr. —— was the husband of a
lady who had been reared from early childhood by
Mrs. Martineau, having been adopted by her simply in
order to provide her little daughter, Ellen, who was

nine years younger than Harriet, with a child companion somewhat about her own age. This lady, her
widowed husband tells me, retained always a most
warm admiration and affection for Mrs. Martineau.
Mothers who have brought up eight children of their
own can appreciate the self-devotedness of this mother
in receiving a ninth child by adoption in order to
increase the well-being of her own little daughter.

Several other instances were told to me of Mrs.
Martineau's benevolence and kindness of disposition.
Young men belonging to her religious body, and living
in lodgings in Norwich, were uniformly made welcome
to her house, as a home, every Sunday evening. One
of the Norwich residents, with whom I have talked
about her, received a presentation from her to the
Unitarian Free School, and afterwards, in his school
life, met with constant encouragement and patronage
at her hands. He tells me that he has never forgotten the stately and impressive address with which
she gave him the presentation ticket, concluding with
a reminder that if he made good use of this opportunity
he might even hope one day to become a Member of
the Town Council of that city,—and at that giddy
eminence her *protégé* now stands.

For the sake of the lesson, it should be understood
that she was thus truly benevolent and kindly, and no
vulgar termagant or scold. It is for us to see how
such a nature can be spoiled for daily life by too un-
checked a course of arbitrary rule, and by repression
of outward signs of tenderness.

Not the least evil which a stern parent, who main-
tains a reserve of demeanour, and who requires strict-
ness of discipline within the home, may do to himself
and his children, is that by denying expression to the

children's feelings he closes to himself the possibility
of knowing what goes on in their young minds. Thus,
a child so restrained may for years suffer under a
sense of injustice, and of undue favouritism shown to
another, or under a belief that the parent's love is
lacking, when a few words might have cleared away the
misapprehension, and given the child the natural
happiness of its age.

Speaking of her childhood, Harriet says: "I had a
devouring passion for justice; justice, first, to my own
precious self, and then to other oppressed people.
Justice was precisely what was least understood in our
house, in regard to servants and children. Now and
then I desperately poured out my complaints; but in
general I brooded over my injuries and those of others
who dared not speak, and then the temptation to
suicide was very strong."

The most vivid picture that she has drawn of the
discipline under which such emotions were induced in
her is found in a story, *The Crofton Boys*, which she
wrote during a severe illness, and under the impression
that it would contain her last words uttered through
the press. Mrs. Proctor, in *The Crofton Boys*, is depicted with remarkable vividness by a series of little
touches, and in a succession of trivial details, with an
avoidance of direct description, that reminds us of the
method of Jane Austen. Harriet never achieved any
other portrait of a character such as this one; for
this is treated with such minute fidelity, and such
evident unconsciousness, that we feel sure, as we
sometimes do with a picture, that the likeness must
be an exact one. So distinct an individuality is shown
to us, and at the same time, the evidences of the
artist's close and careful observation of his model are

so obvious, that, without having seen the subject, we *feel* the accuracy of the likeness. So does the "portrait of a mother" in that tale which Harriet wrote for her last words through the press, show us the nature of Mrs. Martineau in her maternal relation.

"Mrs. Proctor so seldom praised anybody, that her words of esteem went a great way. . . . Everyone in the house was in the habit of hiding tears from Mrs. Proctor, who rarely shed them herself, and was known to think that they might generally be suppressed, and should be so."

If any person were weak enough to express emotion in this way in her presence, Mrs. Proctor would promptly and sternly intimate her disapproval of such indulgence of the feelings. When the little lad was leaving home for the first time, all the rest of the household became a little unhappy over the parting.

"Susan came in about the cord for his box, and her eyes were red,—and at the sight of her Agnes began to cry again ; and Jane bent down over the glove she was mending for him, and her needle stopped.

"'Jane,' said her mother, gravely, 'if you are not mending that glove, give it to me. It is getting late.'

"Jane brushed her hand across her eyes, and stitched away again. Then she threw the gloves to Hugh without looking at him, and ran to get ready to go to the coach."

So little allowance was ordinarily made in that house for signs of affection, or manifestations of personal attachment, that the child who was going away for six months was "amazed to find that his sisters were giving up an hour of their lessons, that they might go with him to the coach." Even when Hugh

got his foot so crushed that it had to be amputated,
though his mother came to him, and gave him every
proper attention, yet " Hugh saw no tears from
her "; nothing more than that " her face was very
pale and grave." His anticipations of her coming
had not been warm ; his one anxiety had been that
he might bear his pain resolutely before her. " As
Hugh cried, he said he bore it so very badly he
did not know what his mother would say if she saw
him." And it was well that he had not anticipated any
outburst of pity or expression of sympathy from her,
for, when she did come, " she kissed him with a long,
long kiss ; but she did not speak." Her first words
in the hearing of her agonised child were spoken to
give him an intimation that the surgeons were waiting
to take off his foot. The boy's reply was—not to cling
to her for support, and to nestle in her bosom for
comfort in the most terrible moment of his young
life, but—" Do not stay now : this pain is *so* bad !  I
can't bear it well at all.  Do go, now, and bid them
make haste, will you ? "

Later, when the leg was better, the poor boy's
mental misery once overpowered him, even in his
mother's presence.  Sitting with her and his sister—

" . . . He said, 'He did not know how he should
bear his misfortune  When he thought of the long,
long days, and months, and years, to the end of his
life, and that he should never run and play, and never
be like other people, and never able to do the com-
monest things without labour and trouble, he wished
he was dead.  He had rather have died !'  Agnes
thought he must be miserable indeed if he would
venture to say this to his mother."  Such was the idea
that these children had of maternal sympathy and

love! So little did they look upon their mother as the one person above all others to whom their secret troubles should be opened!

It is proper to observe that the mother came out of this test well. There is no record that Mrs. Martineau was ever found wanting in due care for her children when the pent-up agony of their bodies or spirits became so violent as to burst the bonds of reserve that her general demeanour and method of management imposed upon them. Her children's misery (for Harriet was not the only one of the family whose childhood was wretched) came not from any intentional neglect, or even from any indifference on her part to their comfort and happiness, but solely, let it be repeated, from her arbitrary manner and her quickness of temper. It is worth repeating (if biography be of value for the lessons which may be drawn from it for the conduct of other lives) that the mother whose children were so spirit-tossed and desolate was, nevertheless, one who gave herself up to their interests, and laboured incessantly and unselfishly for their welfare. It was not love that really was wanting; far less was it faithfulness in the performance of a mother's material duties to her children; all that was lacking was the free play of the emotions on the surface, the kisses, the loving phrases, the fond tones, which are assuredly neither weaknesses nor works of supererogation in family life. By means of candid expression alone can the emotions of one mind touch those of another; and from the lack of such contact between a child and its mother there must come, in so close a life relationship, misery to the younger and disappointment to the elder of the two.

"I really think," says Harriet, "if I had once con-

ceived that anybody cared for me, nearly all the sins
and sorrows of my anxious childhood would have been
spared me." Yet, not only was she well fed, well
clothed, well educated, and sent to amusements to give
her pleasure (magic lanterns, parties, and sea-side trips
are all mentioned); but besides all this, when she did
burst forth, like Hugh Proctor in the book, with the
expression of her suffering, she was soothed and cared
for. But this last happened so rarely—of course
entirely because it was made so difficult for her to express herself—that the occasions lived in her memory
all her life.

The moral consequences of all this were naturally
bad. Even with all motherly sympathy and encouragement, so sickly a child would have been likely to suffer
from timidity, and to fall into occasional fits of de-
spondency and irritability; but, with fear continually
excited in her mind, and with an eternal storm of
passionate opposition to arbitrary authority raging in
her soul, it is no wond. r that the poor child made for
herself a character for wilfulness and obstinacy, while
internally she suffered dreadfully from her conscience.
" In my childhood," she says, " I would assert or deny
anything to my mother that would bring me through
most easily. . . . This was so exclusively to one
person that, though there was remonstrance and
punishment, I was never regarded as a liar in the
family." Her strength of will was very great; and
when she had been placed in a false position by her
dread of rebuke, the powerful will came into play to
maintain a dogged, stubborn, indifferent appearance.
Yet all the while her conscientiousness—the strong
convictions as to what was right, and the ardent desire
to do it, which marked her whole career—was at work

within her, causing a mental shame and distress which might have been easily aided by gentle treatment to overcome the fear and the firmness which were acting together to make her miserable and a sinner.

It is altogether a sad story, but I have not told it at length without reason. The fact that other children are suffering similarly every day makes the record worth repeating. But, besides this, her vivid remembrance of her childish pangs tends to show how warm and strong were her natural affections. If Harriet Martineau's mind had not been sensitive and emotional, and if her love for those united to her by family ties had not been ardent, she would not have felt as she did in her childhood, and she would not have remembered, all through her life, how she had suffered in her early years from unsatisfied affection. Now, this soft, loving, emotional side of her character must be recognised before her life and her work can be properly appreciated.

The intellectual influences of her home life were not more happy than the moral ones. She was thought by her family anything but a clever child. Indeed, Dr. James Martineau (whose recollections are peculiarly valuable, both from his nearness to Harriet in age and from their great attachment in early life) still thinks that she really was a dull child. Her intelligence, he believes, awoke only in her later youth, coincidentally with some improvement in health. It is hard to guess what the impression of her childish intellectual powers might have been under different conditions. She suggestively remarks* :—" It should never be forgotten that the happier a child is the cleverer he will be.

---

\* *Household Education*, p. 202.

This is not only because in a state of happiness the mind is free, and at liberty for the exercise of its faculties instead of spending its thoughts and energy in brooding over troubles, but also because the action of the brain is stronger when the frame is in a state of hilarity; the ideas are more clear, impressions of outward objects are more vivid, and the memory will not let them slip." Moreover, it is a fact worthy of note that the recognition by her family of her mental development followed upon her return home after she had been away for a time, and had been learning at a boarding-school under "the first person of whom she never felt afraid." Still, the fact remains that Harriet was the ugly duckling of her family, and supposed to be the most stupid of the group of Martineau children.

She was active-minded enough, however, to begin early that spontaneous self-education which only intellects of real power undertake, either in childhood or in later years.

Milton was her master. When she was seven years old she came by accident upon a copy of *Paradise Lost* lying open upon a table. Taking it up, she saw the heading "Argument," and in the text her eye caught the word "Satan." Instantly the mind which her relations thought so sluggish was fired by the desire to know how Satan could be argued about. She sought the passage which tells how the arch-fiend was—

> Hurled headlong flaming from the ethereal sky,
> With hideous ruin and combustion, down
> To bottomless perdition, there to dwell
> In adamantine chains and penal fire.

For the ensuing seven years her thoughts dwelt

daily in the midst of the solemn scenes, and moved to the sound of the sonorous music of Milton's poetry. "I wonder how much of it I knew by heart—enough to be always repeating it to myself with every change of light and darkness, and sound, and silence, the moods of the day and the seasons of the year." The dull child, who neglected her multiplication-table, did so because her mind was pre-occupied with thoughts of this grander order.

Her love of books increased, and her range of reading became wide. Milton, although the favourite, was by no means her only beloved author. She read rapidly, and, as clever children often do, voraciously. Whole pages or scenes from Shakespeare, Goldsmith, Thomson, and Milton she learned by heart, until she knew enough poetry to have fitted her for the occupation of a wandering reciter. In this way her self-education in the English classics, and in literary style, went on at the same time with her daily education by living teachers.

Harriet's formal education was somewhat desultory; but it is a noteworthy fact that it was, so far as it went, what would have then been called a "boy's education." In this respect the history of her mental development is the same as that of many other illustrious women of the past. Girls' High Schools, and University examinations for young women, are products of the present day, and are rapidly rendering obsolete the old ideas about the necessary differences and distinctions between the education of boys and girls. But up to the first quarter of this century, the minds of boys and of girls were commonly submitted to entirely different courses of training. While the boys learned precision in reasoning from mathematics,

the girls were considered sufficiently equipped for their
lot in life by a knowledge of the first three rules of
arithmetic.   While any faculty of language that a lad
possessed was trained and exercised by the study of
the classics, his sister was thought to require no more
teaching in composition and grammar than would
enable her to write a letter.  Elaborate samplers,
specimens of fine stitching, of hemming done by a
thread on the most delicate cambric, of marking in
tiny stitches and wonderful designs, and of lace more
noticeable for difficulty in the doing than for beauty,
have come down to us from our grandmothers' days, to
show us how the school-time of the girls was being disposed of, while the boys were studying Euclid, Virgil,
and Homer.   If we have changed all that, and are now
beginning to give a considerable proportion of our
girls the same mental diet for the growth and susten-
ance of their minds with that which is supplied to boys,
it is largely owing to the direct efforts in favour of
such a course put forth by women such as Harriet
Martineau, who had themselves been, at least partially,
educated  "like boys," and were conscious that to
such education they owed much of their mental superiority over average women.

In her earlier years Harriet was taught at home by
her elder brothers and sisters, with the addition of
lessons in some subjects from masters.  She was well
grounded in this manner in Latin, French, and the
ordinary elementary subjects.   But her systematic
education did not begin until she was eleven, when
she and her sister Rachel were sent to a school kept
by a good master, at which boys also were receiving
their education.

The school-life was delectable to Harriet.   Mr.

Perry, the master, was gentle in his manner, and methodical in his style of teaching; and under his tuition the shy, nervous child felt for the first time encouraged to do her best, and aided not merely to learn her lessons, but also to expand her mental faculties. The two years that she remained at Mr. Perry's school gave her a fair insight into Latin and French, and enabled her to discover that arithmetic was to her mind a delightful pastime rather than a difficult study. English composition was formally and carefully taught. This was Harriet's favourite lesson; but she would spend her play-time in covering a slate with sums for the mere pleasure of the exercise.

When Harriet had been at this school for about two years, Mr. Perry left Norwich. The home system of education was then resumed. She had visiting masters in Latin, French, and music. For the rest, Mrs. Martineau selected a course of reading on history, biography, and literature. One of the girls read aloud daily while the others did needle-work.

"The amount of time we spent in sewing now appears frightful; but it was the way in those days among people like ourselves." Harriet became a thoroughly accomplished needle-woman. She had, indeed, a liking for the occupation, and continued to do much of it all through her life. Many of her friends can show handsome pieces of fancy-work done by her hands. Again and again she contributed to public objects by sending a piece of her own beautiful needle-work to be sold for the benefit of a society's funds. Not even in the busiest time of her literary life did she ever entirely cease to exercise her skill in this feminine occupation. In fact, she made wool-work her artistic recreation.

But with all her liking for needle-work, and with all
the use that she made of her skill in the art, she did
feel very keenly how much her time and strength had
been wasted in childhood upon the practice of this
mechanical occupation, that should have been employed
in the cultivation of her mental powers.  A girl then
was required to become a proficient in the making of
every kind of garment.  It was considered a good test
of her capacity to know at an early age how to cut out
and put together a shirt for her father; drawing
threads to cut it by, and drawing threads to do the
rows of fine stitching by, and stitching evenly and
regularly, only two threads of the finest material being
taken for each stitch !  The expenditure of time out of
a girl's life, involved in making her capable of doing
all this, was something shocking.  In these days,
when the development of the means of communica-
tion has made division of labour more generally
practicable than of old, and when nearly all men
and women, from the richest to the artizan classes,
wear garments made chiefly by machinery, I doubt if
many readers can be got to realise how much a girl's
intellectual training was diminished when Harriet Martineau was a child by the vast amount of time con-
sumed in training her as a sempstress.  Harriet was
taught how to make all her own clothes, even to
covering shoes with silk for dancing, and to plaiting
straw bonnets.  It is as though every boy were taught
in his school-life to be a thorough carpenter, so as
to be able, in youth, to turn out unaided any article of
furniture.  It is obvious how much time such technical
training must swallow up.  To conceive how a girl was
held back by it, we must ask ourselves : what was her
brother doing while she was learning needle-work ?

The matter did not end with the waste of time alone. Health, strength, and nerve-force—in a word, *power*—was squandered upon it to a degree truly lamentable. Harriet Martineau's testimony* upon this point may be taken, because of her real fondness for the employment and the skill which she displayed in it :—

"I believe it is now generally agreed, among those who know best, that the practice of sewing has been carried much too far for health, even in houses where there is no poverty or pressure of any kind. No one can well be more fond of sewing than I am; and few, except professional sempstresses, have done more of it ; and my testimony is that it is a most hurtful occupation, except where great moderation is observed. I think it is not so much the sitting and stooping posture as the incessant monotonous action and position of the arms, that causes such wear and tear. Whatever it may be, there is something in prolonged sewing which is remarkably exhausting to the strength, and irritating beyond endurance to the nerves. The censorious gossip, during sewing, which was the bane of our youth," she adds, "wasted more of our precious youthful powers and dispositions than any repentance and amendment in after life could repair."

Harriet's reading for pleasure in childhood had mostly to be done by snatches. She learned much poetry by keeping the book under her work, on her lap, and glancing at a line now and another then. Shakespeare she first enjoyed, while a child, by stealing away from table in the evenings of one winter, and reading by the light of the drawing-room fire, while

* *Household Education*, p. 286.

the rest lingered over dessert in the dining-room. In this way, too, she had to read the newspaper.

The older she grew, the less time was afforded her from domestic duties for study. She was sent, at the age of fourteen, to a boarding-school near Bristol, kept by an aunt of her own, where she stayed fifteen months; and on her return home, her education was considered finished. Thenceforth, it was a struggle to obtain permission to spend any time in reading or writing; and such opportunities as she got, or could make, had to be taken advantage of in secresy.

It is melancholy to read of her " spending a frightful amount of time in sewing," and being " expected always to sit down in the parlour to sew," instead of studying; of her being " at the work-table regularly after breakfast,—making my own clothes, or the shirts of the household, or about some fancy work; or if ever I shut myself into my own room for an hour of solitude, I knew it was at the risk of being sent for to join the sewing-circle "; and of the necessity that she lay under to find time for study by stealing secret hours from sleep. But it is needful to lay stress upon these hindrances through which the growing girl fought her way to mental development. Wide though her knowledge was, great though her mental powers became, who can tell how much was taken from her possibilities (as from those of all other great women of the past) by such waste of her powers in childhood and youth?

It is distressing to think about; the only comfort is that it was inevitable. Of all the causes that unite to make the women of the present more favourably circumstanced than those of the past, none is more potent than the progress of mechanical discovery having relieved them from the necessity of making all the clothing of mankind with their own hands. From the era when Errina, the Greek poetess, mournfully lamented that her mother tied her to her distaff, down to the days in which Harriet Martineau studied by snatches, and spent her days in making shirts in the parlour, an enormous amount of feminine power has been squandered wastefully in this direction. If women hereafter draw out a Comtist calendar of days upon which to reverence the memory of those who have helped them on in the scale of beings, assuredly they must find places for the inventors of the spinning-mule, the stocking-loom, and the sewing-machine.

Religion formed the chief source of happiness to Harriet Martineau in childhood and early youth. Her parents were Unitarians, and their child's theology was, therefore, of a mild type, lacking a hell, a personal devil, a theory of original sin, and the like. She did not fear God, while she feared almost all human beings, and her devotion was thus a source of great joy and little misery.

When she was at the Bristol boarding-school, she came under the ministerial influence of the great Unitarian preacher, the Rev. Dr. Carpenter. The power of his teaching increased the ardour of her religious sentiments. She was just at an intense age —between fourteen and sixteen. Dr. Carpenter's religious instructions made the theism in which she had been educated become a firm personal conviction, and caused the natural action of a sensitive conscience, the self-devotion and humility of a deep power of veneration, and the truthfulness and sincerity of a rare courage, to be blended indistinguishably in their exercise with emotional outpourings of the spirit in worship, and with attachment to certain theological tenets.

Her younger sister well remembers that Harriet's fervent and somewhat gloomy piety was the cause of a good deal of quizzing amongst her elders, when she returned home from Bristol; their amusement being mixed, however, with much respect for her sincerity and conscientiousness. But, as her mind expanded, she thought as well as felt about her theology, and her religious development did not end with childhood.

# CHAPTER II.

EARLY WOMANHOOD : DEVELOPING INFLUENCES.

OLD Norwich, in the early years of this century, was
a somewhat exceptional place.   It so chanced that
besides the exclusiveness natural even now to the society
of a cathedral town—besides the insular tone of
thought and manners which most towns possessed in
those pre-railway days, and while our continental wars
were holding our country-people isolated from foreign
nations—besides all this, Norwich then prided herself
upon having produced a good deal of literary ability.
Her William Taylor was considered to be almost the
only German scholar in England, and other men, whose
names are now nearly forgotten, but who in their day
were looked up to as lights of learning and literature—
Sayers, Smith, Enfield, Alderson, and others,—gave a
tone to the society of Norwich, which, if somewhat
pedantic, was, nevertheless, favourable to the intellectual life.   It is no small testimony to the healthy
and stimulating mental atmosphere of old Norwich
that there successively came out from her, in an age
when individuality and intellect in woman were steadily

repressed, three women of such mark as Amelia Opie,
Elizabeth Fry, and Harriet Martineau.

But even in Norwich the repression just alluded to
was felt by women. Even there it was held, to say
the least, peculiar and undesirable for a girl to wish
to study deep subjects. " When I was young," Miss
Martineau writes, " it was not thought proper for
young ladies to study very conspicuously ; and especially with pen in hand." They were required to be
always ready " to receive callers, without any sign of
blue-stockingism which could be reported abroad.
My first studies in philosophy were carried on with
great care and reserve. . . . I won time for what my
heart was set upon either in the early morning or late
at night."

It was thus at unseasonable hours, and without the
encouraging support of that public feeling of the value
and desirability of knowledge, and the honourableness
of its acquisition, by which a young man's studies are
unconsciously aided, that Harriet in her young womanhood continued to learn. She read Latin with her
brother James, and translated from the classics by
herself. Her cousin, Mr. Lee, read Italian with her
and her sister ; and in course of time they undertook
the translation of Petrarch's sonnets into English verse.
She read Blair's Rhetoric repeatedly. Her Biblical
studies were continued until she was in that position
which, according to Macaulay, is necessary " for a
critic of the niceties of the English language " ; she
had " the Bible at her fingers' ends."

But her solitary studies went also into heavier and
less frequented paths. Dr. Carpenter had taught her to
interest herself in mental and moral philosophy. She
read about these subjects at first because he had

written upon them, and afterwards because she found them really congenial to her mind. Locke and Hartley were the authors whom she studied most closely. Then the works of Priestley, and the study of his life and opinions—which she naturally undertook, be-cause Dr. Priestley was the great Apostle and Martyı of Unitarianism—led her to make a very full acquain-tance with the metaphysicians of the Scotch school.

To how much purpose she thus read the best books then available, upon some of the highest topics that can engage the attention, soon became apparent when she began to write; but of this I must speak in due course later on. Two other of the most important events, or rather trains of events, in the history of her young womanhood, must be mentioned first.

The earlier of these was the gradual on-coming and increase of her deafness. She began to be slightly deaf while she was at Mr. Perry's school, and the fact was there recognised so far as to cause her to be placed next to her teacher in the class. How keenly she even then felt this loss, she has in part revealed in the story of Hugh Procter; and a few lines from an essay of hers on Scott may here be added :

" Few have any idea of the all-powerful influence which the sense of personal infirmity exerts over the mind of a child. If it were known, its apparent dis-proportionateness to other influences would, to the careless observer, appear absurd; to the thoughtful it would afford new lights respecting the conduct of educational discipline; it would also pierce the heart of many a parent who now believes that he knows all, and who feels so tender a regret for what he knows that even the sufferer wonders at its extent. But this is a species of suffering which can never obtain suffi-

cient sympathy, because the sufferer himself is not
aware, till he has made comparison of this with other
pains, how light all others are in comparison."

As pathetically, but more briefly, she says about
herself :—" My deafness, when new, was the upper-
most thing in my mind day and night."

Her inability to hear continued to increase by slow
degrees during the next six years ; and when she was
eighteen " a sort of accident " suddenly increased it.
Music had, until then, been one of her great delights,
and it shows how gradual was the progress of her deafness, that she found herself able to hear at an orches-
tral concert, provided she could get a seat with a back
against which she could press her shoulder-blades, for
a long time after the music had become inaudible without this assistance.   Such a gradual deprivation of a
most important sense is surely far more trying than
a quick, unexpected, and obviously irremediable loss
would be.   The alternations of hope and despair, the
difficulty of inducing the sufferer's friends to recognise
how serious the case is, the perhaps yet greater difficulty to the patient to resolutely step out of the ranks
of ordinary people and take up the position of one
deficient in a sense, the mortifications which have to
be endured again and again both from the ignorance
of strangers and the mistaken sympathy of friends—
all these make up the special trial of one who becomes
by degrees the subject of a chronic affection.   No
sensitive person can possibly pass through this fiery
trial unchanged.   Such an experience must either
refine or harden ; must either strengthen the powers of
endurance or break down the mind to querulous ill-
temper ; must either make self the centre of creation
or greatly add to the power of putting personal in-

terests aside for the sake of wider and more unselfish thoughts and feelings. Which class of influences Harriet Martineau accepted from her trial the history of her courageous, resolute life-work, and her devotion to truth and duty as she saw them, will sufficiently show.

How much she suffered in mind was quite unknown to her family at the time. She was always reserved in speaking about her own feelings and emotions to her mother, and in this particular case Mrs. Martineau, with the kindest intentions, discouraged, as far as possible, all recognition of the growing infirmity. The society of Norwich had never been very attractive to the young girl, who was above the average in natural abilities, and still further removed from the petty and frivolous gossip of the commonplace evening party, by the extensive and elevating course of study through which her mind had passed. Had she been well able to hear, she could have quietly accepted what such intercourse could give her. This would have been much. Kindliness and good feeling, common sense, and ideas about man and his circumstances, are to be enjoyed and gained quite as much in ordinary as in what is commonly called intellectual society. But in the freshness of her sensitive suffering Harriet shrank from the Norwich evening parties. Her mother, however, insisted upon her taking her full share of visiting.

The case was made worse by the customary errors in the treatment of deaf persons; namely, the endeavouring to keep up the illusion that she was not deaf, the occasional assurances that she could hear as well as ever if it were not for her habits of abstraction, and so forth, and the imploring her to always ask when she did not hear what was said, followed by scoldings (kindly meant, but none the less irritating to the object) when it was found that she had been silently losing the larger part of a conversation. False pride, pretence, and selfish exactions were thus sought to be nourished in her; while the blessings of an open recognition of her trouble, and a full and free sympathy with her pain and her difficulty in learning to bear it, were at the same time withheld.

I have spoken of this method of treatment of such a case as erroneous. But in such a matter only those who have gone through the experience and have come out of it at last, as she did, with the moral nature strengthened, and the power of self-management increased, can be really competent to express an opinion upon the proper method of behaviour to similar sufferers. I hasten to add, therefore, that in substance the view that I have given is that expressed in Harriet Martineau's *Letter to the Deaf*, published in 1834. In that remarkable fragment of autobiography she appealed to the large number of people who suffered like herself, to insist upon the frank recognition of their infirmity, and to themselves acquiesce with patience in all the deprivations and mortifications which the loss of a sense must bring. The revelation in this essay of her own sufferings is most touching; and very noble and beautiful is the way in which she urges that the misery must be met, and the humiliation must be turned aside, by no other means than courage, candour, patience, and an unselfish determination to consider first the convenience and happiness of others instead of the sufferer's own.

"Instead of putting the singularity out of sight we should acknowledge it in words, prepare for it in habits, and act upon it in social intercourse. Thus only can we save others from being uneasy in our presence, and sad when they think of us. That we can thus alone make ourselves sought and beloved is an inferior considera-tion, though an important one to us, to whom warmth and kindness are as peculiarly animating as sunshine to the caged bird. This frankness, simplicity, and cheerfulness can only grow out of a perfect acquiescence in our circumstances. Submission is not enough. Pride fails at the most critical moment. But hearty acquiescence cannot fail to bring forth cheerfulness. The thrill of delight which arises during the ready agreement to profit by pain (emphatically the joy with which no stranger intermeddleth) must subside like all other emotions; but it does not depart without leaving the spirit lightened and cheered; and every visitation leaves it in a more genial state than the last. . . . . I had infinitely rather bear the perpetual sense of privation than become unaware of anything which is true—of my intellectual deficiencies, of my disqualifications for society, of my errors in matter of fact, and of the burdens that I necessarily impose on those who surround me. We can never get beyond the necessity of keeping in full view the worst and the best that can be made of our lot. The worst is either to sink under the trial or to be made callous by it. The best is to be as wise as possible under a great disability, and as happy as possible under a great privation."

It is essential, for a correct understanding of her character, that this great trial of her youth should be presented amidst the moulding influences of that time with as much strength as it was experienced. But it is difficult, within the necessary limits of quotation, to convey an idea to the reader of either the intensity and bitterness of the suffering revealed, or of the firm-ness and beauty of the spirit with which the trial was met. Nor was the advice that she gave to others mere talk, which she herself never put in practice. If her family did not realise at the time how deeply she suffered, still less could her friends in later life discover by anything in her manners that her soul had been so searched and her spirits so tried. So frankly and candidly, and with such an utter absence of affectation, did she accept this condition of her life, that those around her hardly realised that she felt it as a deprivation; and a few lines in her autobiography, in which she mentions how conscious she was of intellectual fatigue from the lack of those distractions to the mind which enter continually through the normal ear, came like a painful shock to her friends, making them feel that they had been unconscious of a need ever present with her throughout life.

For some time after the deafness began, she did not use an ear-trumpet. Like many in a similar position, she persuaded herself that her deafness was not sufficiently great to cause any considerable inconvenience to others in conversation. At length, however, she was enlightened upon this point. An account appeared in a Unitarian paper of two remarkable cures of deafness by galvanism, and Harriet's friends persuaded her to try this new remedy. For a brief while, hope was revived in her; the treatment threw her into a state of nervous fever, during which she regained considerable sensibility in the organ of hearing. The improvement was very temporary, but it lasted sufficiently long to let her know how much her friends had been straining their throats for her sake. From that time she invariably carried and used an ear-trumpet, commencing with an india-rubber tube, with a cup at the end for the speaker to take into his hand, but afterwards employing an ordinary stiff trumpet.

Into this existence, which had hitherto been so full of sadness, there came at length the bright-tinted and vivid shower of light, which means so much to a woman. Love came to brighten the life so dark hitherto for lack of that sunshine. Much as it is to any woman to know herself beloved by the man whom she loves, to Harriet Martineau it was even more than

to most. It was not only that her character was a
strong one, and that to such a nature all influences
that are accepted become powerful forces, but besides
this she had always loved more than she had been
loved ; and her self-esteem had been systematically
suppressed by her mother's stern discipline, and afterwards injured by the mortifications to which the on-
coming of her deafness gave rise. How much, in such
a case, it must have been when the hour at last came
for the history of the heart to be written ! How delightful the time when she could cherish in her
thoughts a love which was at once an equal friendship
and a vivid passion ! How great the revolution in her
mind when she found that the man whom she could
love would choose her from all the world of women to
be his dearest, the partner of his life !

It would be a proof, if proof were needed at this
time of day, that it is well-nigh impossible for any
person to give a candid, full, and unerring record of
his own past, and the circumstances in it which have
most influenced his development, to turn from the
brief and cursory record which Harriet Martineau's
autobiography gives of this attachment, to the complete story as I have it to tell, here and in a future
chapter.

The strongest of all the family affections of her
childhood and youth was that which she felt for her
brother James. He was two years younger than
herself; they had been playmates in childhood, and
companions in study later on. Harriet's first attraction to Mr. Worthington was that he was her brother's
friend. The two young men were fellow students at
college, preparing for the Unitarian ministry. Worthington was already well known to Harriet, from her

brother's letters, before she saw him. He then went
on a visit to Norwich, to spend a part of the vacation
with James, and the interest which the friend and the
sister already felt in each other, from their mutual
affection for the brother, soon ripened into love. This
was, I believe, in 1822, when she was twenty years
old.

Her father and mother looked not unkindly upon
the dawning of this affection. The brother, however,
who knew the two so well, felt quite certain that they
were not suited for each other. Harriet was of a
strong, decided temper, even somewhat arbitrary and
hasty, quick in her judgments, and firm in her opinions.
The temperament of Worthington, on the other hand,
was, I am told, gentle, impressionable, and sensitive
in the extreme. He was highly conscientious, and
ultra-tender in his treatment of the characters and
opinions of others. The two seemed in many respects
the antipodes of each other. He who knew them both
best was convinced that they would not be happy
together; and that opinion he has never changed.

It is above all things difficult to predict beforehand
whether two apparently antagonistic characters will
really clash and jar in the close union of married life;
or whether, on the contrary, the deficiencies of the one
will be supplemented by those opposite tendencies
which are rather in excess in the other. It is notorious that marriages are seldom perfect matches in
the view of outsiders; the incongruities in the tem-
peraments and the habits of life and thought, are more
easily discerned than the fusing influence of ardent love
can be measured. Nor, indeed, can the changes which
will be worked in the disposition by a surrender to the
free play of emotion be accurately foreseen. Consi-

derations such as these, however, do not have much
weight in the mind of a young man whose experience
of the mysteries of the human heart is yet to come ;
and James Martineau was strongly averse to the engagement of his sister and his friend. Their attachment was not then permitted to become an engagement.
Worthington was poor—was still only a student,—
Harriet was supposed, at that time, to be well por-
tioned ; the sensitive temperament of the young lover
felt the variety of discouragements placed in the path of
his affection ; and so that affection which should have
brought only joy became, in fact, to Harriet the cause
of sorrow, suspense, and anxiety. Yet its vivifying
influence was felt ; and the true happiness which is
inseparable from mutual love, however the emotion be
checked and denied its full expression, was not lacking.
For some insight into what Harriet Martineau knew
and felt of love, we must look elsewhere than in the
formal record of the Autobiography.* But this, like
all the other chief events of her life, has found a place
in her works under a thin veiling of her personality.
Let us see from one of her early essays, how Harriet

* Mr. H. G. Atkinson writes to me : " She had written much
more at length [than is published] in her Autobiography about her
courtship ; but she consulted me about publishing it, and I advised
her not to do so—the matter counted for so little in such a life as
hers." The quotation which I give here shows for what it did
really count in the history of her mental development. But so
difficult must it needs be for the writer of an autobiography to
speak frankly of the more sacred experiences of the life, that it is
not surprising that Harriet Martineau " destroyed what she had
written," when so advised by the friend whom she consulted. I
need only add that the many new details about the facts of this
matter, which I am able to give, I have received from two of her
own generation, both of whom were very intimate friends of hers
at the time when all this occurred.

Martineau learned to regard love. The essay is called,
" In a Hermit's Cave.'

The place was not ill-chosen by the holy man, if the circumstances could but have been adapted to that highest worship—the
service of the life. . . . But there is yet wanting the altar of the
human heart, on which alone a fire is kindled from above to shine
in the faces of all true worshippers for ever. Where this flame,
the glow of human love, is burning, there is the temple of worship,
be it only beside the humblest village hearth : where it has not
been kindled there is no sanctuary ; and the loftiest amphitheatre
of mountains, lighted up by the ever-burning stars, is no more the
dwelling-place of Jehovah than the Temple of Solomon before it
was filled with the glory of the Presence. . . .

Yes, Love is worship, authorised and approved. . . . Many are
the gradations through which this service rises until it has reached
that on which God has bestowed His most manifest benediction,
on which Jesus smiled at Cana, but which the devotee presumed
to decline. Not more express were the ordinances of Sinai than
the Divine provisions for wedded love ; never was it more certain
that Jehovah benignantly regarded the festivals of His people than
it is daily that He appointed those mutual rejoicings of the
affections, which need but to be referred to Him to become a holy
homage. Yet there have been many who pronounce common that
which God has purified, and reject or disdain that which He has
proffered and blest. How ignorant must such be of the growth of
that within ! How unobservant of what passes without ! Would
that all could know how from the first flow of the affections, until
they are shed abroad in their plenitude, the purposes of creation
become fulfilled. Would that all could know how, by this mighty
impulse, new strength is given to every power; how the intellect
is vivified and enlarged ; how the spirit becomes bold to explore
the path of life, and clear-sighted to discern its issues. . . . For
that piety which has humanity for its object—must not that
heart feel most of which tenderness has become the element ?
must not the spirit which is most exercised in hope and fear be
most familiar with hope and fear wherever found ?

How distinctly I saw all this in those who are now sanctifying
their first Sabbath of wedded love. . . . The one was at peace
with all that world which had appeared so long at war with him.
He feared nothing, he possessed all ; and of the overflowings of
his love he could spare to every living thing. The other thought
of no world but the bright one above, and the quiet one before

her, in each of which dwelt one in whom she had perfect trust.
. . . In her the progression has been so regular, and the work so
perfect, that any return to the former perturbations of her spirit
seems impossible. She entered upon a new life when her love
began; and it is as easy to conceive that there is one Life Giver
to the body, and another to the spirit, as that this progression is
not the highest work of God on earth, and its results abounding
to His praise. . . . To those who know them as I know them,
they appear already possessed of an experience in comparison with
which it would appear little to have looked abroad from the Andes,
or explored the treasure-caves of the deep, or to have conversed
with every nation under the sun. If they could see all that the
eyes of the firmament look upon, and hear all the whispered
secrets that the roving winds bear in their bosoms, they could
learn but little new; for the deepest mysteries are those of human
love, and the vastest knowledge is that of the human heart.

Even more vividly, at a later period, she told something of her experiences in one of her fictions, under
the guise of a conversation between a young husband
and wife :—

"Do you really think there are any people that have passed
through life without knowing what that moment was, that stir in
one's heart on being first sure that one is beloved? It is most
like the soul getting free of the body and rushing into Paradise,
I should think. Do you suppose anybody ever lived a life without
having felt this?"

Walter feared it might be so; but, if so, a man missed the
moment that made a man of one that was but an unthinking creature
before; and a woman the moment best worth living for. . . .

"It seems to me," said Effie, "that though God has kindly
given this token of blessedness to all or to so many that we
may nearly say all without distinction of great or humble, rich
or poor, the great and the lowly use themselves to the opposite
faults. The great do not seem to think it the most natural thing
to marry where they first love; and the lowly are too ready to
love."

"That is because the great have too many things to look to
besides love; and the lowly have too few. The rich have their
lighted palaces to bask in, as well as the sunshine; and they
must have a host of admirers, as well as one bosom friend. And
when the poor man finds that there is one bliss that no power on

earth can shut him out from, and one that drives out all evils for
the time—one that makes him forget the noonday heats, and one
that tempers the keen north wind, and makes him walk at his
full height when his superiors lounge past him in the street—no
wonder he is eager to meet it, and jogs the time-glass to make
it come at the soonest. If such a man is imprudent, I had
rather be he than one that first let it slip through cowardice, and
would then bring it back to gratify his low ambition!"

"And for those who let it go by for conscience sake, and do
not ask for it again?"

"Why, they are happy in having learned what *the one feeling
is that life is worth living for.* They may make themselves happy
upon it for ever, after that. O Effie, you would not believe,
nothing could make you believe, what I was the day before and
the day after I saw that sudden change of look of yours that told
me all. The one day, I was shrinking inwardly from everything I
had to do, and every word of my father's, and everybody I met:
and was always trying to make myself happy in myself alone,
with the sense of God being near me and with me. The other
day, I looked down upon everybody, in a kindly way; and yet
I looked up to them too, for I felt a respect that I never knew
before for all that were suffering and enjoying; and I felt as if I
could have brought the whole world nearer to God, if they would
have listened to me. I shall never forget the best moment of
all—when my mind had suddenly ceased being in a great tumult,
which had as much pain as pleasure in it. When I said distinctly
to myself, 'She loves me,' Heaven came down round about me that
minute."[*]

This tells how Harriet Martineau could love in her
youth. Perhaps the stream ran all the more power-
fully for its course being checked; for it was over three
years after she met and became attached to Mr. Worthington before their love was allowed to be declared,
and their engagement was permitted—a long period
for hope and fear to do their painful office in the soul,
a long test of the reality of the love on both sides.

---

[*] *Illustrations of Political Economy :* " A Tale of the Tyne,"
pp. 54, *et seq.* This passage is doubly interesting from the fact
that Mr. Malthus, the discoverer of the Population Law, sent
specially to thank her for having written it.

Her extensive and deep studies, her sufferings and inward strivings from her deafness, and the joys and anxieties of her love, were the chief moulding influences of her early womanhood. We shall soon see how she came to seek expression for the results of all these in literature.

# CHAPTER III.

### EARLIEST WRITINGS.

HARRIET MARTINEAU's first attempt to write for publication was made in the same year that her acquaintance with Mr. Worthington was formed; in 1822, when she was twenty years old. It was, apparently, at the close of the vacation in which Worthington had visited his friend Martineau at Norwich, that she commenced a paper with the design of offering it to the Unitarian magazine, *The Monthly Repository*. She had told James that when he had returned to college she should be miserable, and he had, with equal kindness and sense, advised her to try to forget her feelings about the parting by an attempt at authorship. On a bright September morning, therefore, when she had seen him start by the early coach, soon after six, she sat down in her own room with a supply of foolscap paper before her to write her first article.

The account which she—writing from memory—gives in her autobiography, of this little transaction, is curiously inaccurate, as far as the trifling details are concerned. Her own statement is that she took the letter " V " for her signature, and that she found her

paper printed in the next number of the magazine,
" and in the 'Notices to Correspondents' a request to
hear more from ' V,' of Norwich." Her little errors
about these facts must be corrected, because the truth
of the matter is at once suggestive and amusing.

The article may be found in the *Monthly Repository*
for October, 1822. It is signed, not " V," but
" Discipulus." This, it need hardly be pointed out,
is the *masculine* form of the Latin for learner, or
apprentice. The note in the correspondents' column
is not in that same month's magazine ; but in the
number for the succeeding month, the editor says in
his answers to correspondents : " The continuation of
' Discipulus' has come to hand. *His* other proposed
communications will probably be acceptable." If
more proofs than these were required that the youthful
authoress had presented herself to her editor in a
manly disguise, it would be furnished by a passage in
one of these " Discipulus " articles, in which she defi-
nitely figures herself as a masculine writer, speaking
of " our sex " (*i.e.* the male sex) as a man would do.
The interesting fact is thus disclosed that Harriet
Martineau adds another to the group of the most
eminent women writers of this century who thought it
necessary to assume the masculine sex in order to
obtain a fair hearing and an impartial judgment for
their earliest work. Surely, as our " Discipulus "
takes her place in this list with George Eliot, George
Sand, and Currer, Ellis, and Acton Bell, a great deal
is disclosed to us about how women in the past have
had to make their way to recognition *against the tide*
of public opinion.

That first printed essay is interesting because it was
the precursor of so long a course of literary work,

rather than for itself. Yet it is not without its own
interest, and is very far indeed from being the crude,
imperfect performance of the ordinary amateur. The
subject is "Female Writers of Practical Divinity."
Here are the first words that Harriet Martineau
uttered through the press:

" I do not know whether it has been remarked by
others as well as myself, that some of the finest and
most useful English works on the subject of practical
Divinity are by female authors. I suppose it is owing
to the peculiar susceptibility of the female mind, and
its consequent warmth of feeling, that its productions,
when they are really valuable, find a more ready way
to the heart than those of the other sex; and it gives
me great pleasure to see women gifted with superior
talents applying those talents to promote the cause of
religion and virtue."

There is nothing remarkable in the literary form of
this first article. How soon she came to have a style
of her own, vivid, stirring, and instinct with a powerful individuality, may have been gathered already from
the quotations given in our last chapter. But in her
first paper the style is coldly correct; imitative of
good but severe models, and displaying none of the
writer's individuality. Two points as regards the
matter of the essay are of special interest, and
thoroughly characteristic. It is interesting, in the
first place, to know that she who was destined to do
probably more than any other one woman of her
century for the enlargement of the sphere of her sex in
the field of letters, should have written her first article
on the subject of the capacity of women to teach
through their writings. The second point worth
noticing is that her idea of " practical Divinity " is,

simply, good conduct. Theological disputation and dogma do not disturb her pages. Her view of practical Divinity is that it teaches morals; and it is largely because the women to whose writings she draws attention have occupied themselves with the attempt to trace out rules of conduct, that she is interested in their writings, and rejoices in their labours. Indeed, she only alludes once to the opinions on dogmatic theology of the writers whom she quotes, and then she does it only to put aside with scorn the idea that morality and teaching should be rejected because of differences upon points of theology.

Encouraged by the few stately words with which the editor of the *Repository* had received the offer of more contributions, " Discipulus " continued his literary labours, and the result appeared in a paper on " Female Education," published in the *Monthly Repository* of February, 1823. This is a noble and powerful appeal for the higher education of girls, and the full development of all the powers of our sex. It is written with gentleness and tact, but it courageously asserts and demands much that was strange indeed to the tone of that day, though it has become quite commonplace in ours.

The author (supposed to be a man, be it remembered), disclaimed any intention of proving that the minds of women were equal to those of men, but only desired to show that what little powers the female intellect might possess should be fully cultivated. Nevertheless, the fact was pointed out that women had seldom had a chance of showing how near they might be able to equal men intellectually ; for while the lad was at the higher school and college, preparing his mind for a future, " the girl is probably confined to low pursuits, her aspirings after knowledge are subdued, she is taught to believe that solid information is unbecoming her sex; almost her whole time is expended on low accomplishments, and thus, before she is sensible of her powers, they are checked in their growth and chained down to mean objects, to rise no more; and when the natural consequences of this mode of treatment are seen, all mankind agree that the abilities of women are far inferior to those of men." Having shown reasons to believe that women would take advantage of higher opportunities if such were allowed them, "Discipulus" maintained in detail that the cultivation of their minds would improve them for all the accepted feminine duties of life, charitable, domestic, and social, and that the consequent elevation of the female character would react beneficially on the male; cited the works of a cluster of eminent authoresses, as showing that women could think upon "the noblest subjects that can exercise the human mind"; and closed with the following paragraph, wherein occur the phrases by which it is shown that our "Discipulus" of twenty is masquerading as a man, more decisively even than by the termination of the Latin *nom de guerre*.

"I cannot better conclude than with the hope that these examples of what may be done may excite a noble emulation in *their own* sex, and *in ours* such a conviction of the value of the female mind, as shall overcome *our* long-cherished prejudices, and induce *us* to give *our* earnest endeavours to the promotion of *women's* best interests."

It is most interesting to thus discover that Harriet Martineau's first writings were upon that "woman question" which she lived to see make such wonderful advances, and which she so much forwarded, both by her direct advocacy, and by the indirect influence of the proof which she afforded, that a woman may be a thinker upon high topics and a teacher and leader of men in practical politics, and yet not only be irreproachable in her private life, but even show herself throughout it, in the best sense, truly feminine.

Harriet contributed nothing more to the *Monthly Repository* after this (so far as can now be ascertained), for a considerable time. Encouraged by the success of her first attempts with periodicals, she commenced a book of a distinctly religious character, which was issued in the autumn of the same year, 1823, by Hunter, of St. Paul's Churchyard.

The little volume was published anonymously. Its title-page runs thus : " *Devotional Exercises* ; consisting of Reflections and Prayers for the use of Young Persons. To which is added an Address on Baptism. By a Lady."

The character of the work is, perhaps, sufficiently indicated by the title. But it would be a mistake to suppose that the book is a commonplace one. It contains a good deal of dogmatising, and many platitudes. It contains likewise, however, many a noble thought and many a high aspiration, expressed in words equally flowing and fervent. A "Reflection" (something like a short sermon) and a prayer are supplied for each morning and each evening of the seven days of the week. She had already attained to such insight into the human mind as to recognise that religious devotion is an exercise of the emotions. Proof, too, is given in this little work of the fulness with which she realised that true religion must be expressed by service to mankind ; to those nearest to one first, and afterwards to others; and, indeed, that a high sense of social duty, with a fervent and unselfish devotion to it, *is* religion, rather than either the spiritual dram-drinking, or the dogmatic irrationality to which that name of high import is frequently applied.

The prayers in this little volume differ much from the supplications for personal benefits which are commonly called prayers. These are rather aspirations, or meditations. The highest moral attributes, personified in God, are held up for the worship of the imperfect human creature, with fervent aspiration to approach as nearly as may be possible towards that light of unsullied goodness.

The lack of petitions for material benefits which appears in these "Devotions" was by no means unconscious, instinctive, or accidental. She had deliberately given up the practice of praying for personal benefits, partly because she held that, since it is impossible for us to foresee how far our highest interests may be served or hindered by changes in our external circumstances, it is not for us to attempt to indicate, or even to form a desire, as to what those circumstances shall be. As regarded the emotional side of her religion, she had come to prefer to leave herself and her fate to the unquestioned direction of a higher power.

But there was more than this in it. In her philosophical studies, she had, of course, met with the eternal debates of metaphysicians and theologians on Foreknowledge, Fate, and Freedom of the Will. The difficult question had, indeed, presented itself to her active and acute young mind long before those studies began. She remembered that when she was but eleven years old she once found courage to offer her question-

ings upon this point to her elder brother Thomas.
She asked : If God foreknew from eternity all the evil
deeds that every one of us should do in our lives, how
can He justly punish us for those actions, when the
time comes that we are born, and in due course commit
them ?  Her brother replied merely that she was
not yet old enough to understand the point.  The
answer did not satisfy the child.  She knew that if she
were old enough to feel the difficulty, she must also be
mentally fit to receive some kind of explanation.  But,
under the pastoral influence of Dr. Carpenter, the
emotional side of her religion was cultivated, and such
doubts and difficulties of the reason were put away for
the time.

Not for all time, however, could the problem be
shirked by so active, logical, and earnest a mind.  It
recurred to her when she was left to her own spiritual
guidance.  Long before the date of these " Devotions "
she had fought out the battle in her own mind, and
had reached the standpoint from which her Prayers are
written.  She had convinced herself of the truth of the
Necessitarian doctrine, that we are what we are, we
do what we do, because of the impulses given by our
previous training and circumstances ; and that the way
to amend any human beings or all mankind is to
improve their education, and to give them good surroundings and influences, and mental associations : in
short, that physical and psychological phenomena
alike depend upon antecedent phenomena, called
causes.

As soon as she had thus settled her mind in the
doctrine of Necessity, she perceived that prayer, in the
ordinary sense of the term, had become impossible.  If
it be believed that all that happens in the world is the

consequence of the course of the events which have happened before, it is clear that no petitions can alter the state of things at any given moment. A belief in the efficacy of " besieging Heaven with prayers " implies a supposition that a Supreme Ruler of the Universe interferes arbitrarily with the sequence of events. Those whose minds are clear that no such arbitrary interference ever does take place, but that, on the contrary, like events always and invariably follow from like causes, cannot rationally ask for this fundamental rule of the government of the universe to be set aside for their behoof; even although they may believe in an all-powerful Divine Ruler, who has appointed this sequence of events for the law under which His creatures shall live and develop.

Still, however, Harriet Martineau supplicated for spiritual benefits, as we have seen in the little volume of *Devotional Exercises*. These aspirations not only gave her an emotional satisfaction, but were, she then thought, justifiable on necessitarian principles; for each time that we place our minds in a certain attitude we increase their " set " in the same direction; and she believed at that time that a holy life was in this way aided by frequent reflections on and aspirations towards the highest ideal of holiness personified in the name of God.

Her religious belief was, then, pure Theism. To her, it was still very good to be a worshipper of Jehovah, the Eternal Presence, the Ever-living Supreme; and Jesus was His Messenger, the highest type that He had ever permitted to be revealed to man of the excellencies of the divine nature. But there was no Atonement, no personal Evil One, no hell, no verbally-inspired revelation in her creed.

It will be unnecessary to say more about her theological beliefs, till the next twenty years have been recorded; for in that period there was substantially no change in her views. There did come, indeed, a change in her method of self-management, and in her opinions as to the way in which religious feelings should affect daily life. She soon concluded that we are best when least self-conscious about our own goodness, and that, therefore, we should rely upon receiving inspiration to right and elevated feelings from passing influences, and should refrain from putting our minds, by a regular exercise of volition, into affected postures, in anticipation of those high emotions which we cannot command. Under these beliefs she soon ceased all formal prayer. Meantime she was still, at twenty-one years old, in the condition of mind to write *Devotional Exercises*.

The little book met with a favourable acceptance among the Unitarians, and speedily went into the second edition. Thus encouraged, Harriet began another volume of the same character. Such work could not proceed very fast, however; for her domestic duties were not light, and her writing was still looked upon in her family as a mere recreation. She laboured under all the disadvantages of the amateur. But events soon began to crowd into her life to alter this view of the case, and to prepare the way for her beginning to do the work of her life in the only fashion in which such labour can be effectively carried on—as a serious occupation, the principal feature of every day's duties.

After a long period of poverty and distress, caused by the Napoleonic wars, England, in 1824, experienced the special dangers of a time of rapidly increasing wealth. There was more real wealth in the country,

owing to the expansion of trade, which followed on the
reopening of the Continent to our commerce; but
speculation made this development appear far greater
than it was in reality.

There was, at that time, no sort of check upon the
issue of paper money. Not only did the Bank of
England send out notes without limit; not only could
every established bank multiply its drafts recklessly;
but any small tradesman who pleased might embark in
the same business, and put forth paper money without
check or control. Thus there was money in abundance; the rate of interest was low, and prices rose.

The natural and inevitable consequence of this state
of things, at a moment when trade was suddenly revived, was a rage for speculation. Not only merchants
and manufacturers were seized with this epidemic; the
desire for higher profits than could be obtained by
quiet and perfectly safe investments spread amongst
every class. "As for what the speculation was like,
it can hardly be recorded on the open page of history
without a blush. Besides the joint-stock companies
who undertook baking, washing, baths, life insurance,
brewing, coal-portage, wool-growing, and the like,
there was such a rage for steam navigation, canals, and
railroads, that in the session of 1825, 438 petitions for
private Bills were presented, and 286 private Acts were
passed. . . . It is on record that a single share of a
mine, on which £70 had been paid, yielded £200 per
cent., having risen speedily to a premium of £1400
per share."*

Periods of such inflation invariably and necessarily
close in scenes of disaster. Gold becomes scarce;
engagements that have been recklessly entered into

* Harriet Martineau's *History of the Peace*, book ii. p. 8.

cannot be met; goods have been produced in response to a speculative instead of a legitimate demand, and, therefore, will not sell; the locked-up capital cannot be released, nor can it be temporarily supplied, except upon ruinous terms. Panic commences; it spreads over the business world like fire over the dry prairies. The badly-managed banks and the most speculative business houses begin to totter; the weakest of them fall, and the crash brings down others like a house of cards; and in the depreciation of goods and the dis-appearance of capital, the prudent, sagacious, and honourable merchant suffers for the folly, the reckless-ness, the avarice, and the dishonesty of others.

Such a crash came, from such causes, in the early winter of 1825. Harriet Martineau's father was one of those injured by the panic, without having been a party to the errors which produced it. He had resisted the speculative mania, and allowed it to sweep by him to its flood. It was, therefore, by no fault of his own that he was caught by the ebbing wave, and carried backwards, to be stranded in the shallows. His house did not fail; but the struggle was a cruel one for many months. How severe the crisis was may be judged from the fact that between sixty and seventy banks stopped payment within six weeks.

The strain of this business anxiety told heavily upon the already delicate health of Mr. Thomas Martineau. In the early spring of 1826, it became clear that his days were numbered. Up to the commencement of that troubled winter it had been supposed that his daughters would be amply provided for in the event of his death. But so much had been lost in the crisis, that he found himself, in his last weeks, compelled to alter his will, and was only able to leave to his wife and daughters a bare maintenance. He lingered on till June, and in that month he died.

It was while Mr. Martineau lay ill, that Harriet's second book, *Addresses, Prayers, and Hymns,* passed through the press, and the dying father took great interest and found great comfort in his child's work. Much of it he must have read with feelings rendered solemn by his situation.

This little volume so closely resembles the *Devotional Exercises,* that it is unnecessary to refer to it at greater length. The hymns, which are the special feature of this volume, do not call for much notice. They are not quite commonplace; but verse was not Harriet's natural medium of expression: she wrote a considerable quantity of it in her early days, as most young authors do; but she soon came to see for herself that her gift of expression in its most elevated form was rather that which makes the orator than the poet.

The comparative poverty to which the family were reduced on Mr. Martineau's death, at once freed Harriet, to a considerable extent, from the obstacles which had previously been interposed to her spending time in writing. It was still far from being recognised that literature was to be her profession; but it was obvious that if her pen could bring any small additions to her income they would be very serviceable. A friend gave her an introduction to Mr. Houlston, then publishing at Wellington, Shropshire; and a few little tales, which she had lying by, were offered to him. He accepted them, issued them in tiny volumes, and paid her five guineas for the copyright of each story. This, then, was the beginning of Harriet Martineau's professional authorship.

# CHAPTER IV.

## GRIEF STRUGGLE AND PROGRESS.

The loss of pecuniary position did something more for Harriet Martineau besides opening the way to work in literature. The knowledge that she was now poor gave her lover courage to declare himself, and to seek her for his wife. Poverty, therefore, brought her that experience which is so much in a woman's mental history, however little it, perhaps, goes for in a man's. A love in youth, fervent, powerful, and pure; a love, happy and successful in the essential point that it is reciprocated by its object, however fate may deny it outward fruition; such a love, once filling a woman's soul, sweetens it and preserves it for her whole life through. Pity the shrivelled and decayed old hearts which were not thus embalmed in youth! Harriet Martineau did have this precious experience; and her womanliness of nature remained fresh and true and sweet to the end of her days because of it.

There may be many married women old maids in heart—to be so is the punishment of those who marry without love; and there are many, like Harriet Martineau, who are single in life, but whose hearts have been mated, and so made alive. I do not know that she would have gained by marriage, in any way, except in the chance of motherhood, a yet greater fact than love itself to a woman. On the other hand, her work must have been hindered by the duties of married life, even if her marriage had been thoroughly happy, and her lot free from exceptional material cares. Matronage is a profession in itself. The duties of a wife and mother, as domestic life is at present arranged, absorb much time and strength, and so diminish the possibilities of intellectual labour. Moreover, the laws regulating marriage are still, and fifty years ago were far more, in a very bad state ; and, leaving a woman wholly dependent for fair treatment, whether as a wife or mother, upon the mercy and goodness of the man she marries, justify Harriet Martineau's observation : " The older I have grown, the more serious have seemed to me the evils and disadvantages of married life, as it exists among us at this time." The wife who is beloved and treated as an equal partner in life, the mother whose natural rights in the guardianship of her family are respected, the mistress of a home in which she is the sunshine of husband and children, must ever be the happiest of women. But far better is it to be as Harriet Martineau was—a widow of the heart by death—than to have the affections torn through long years by neglect and cruelty, springing less from natural badness than from the evil teaching of vile laws and customs. Fifty years ago marriage was a dangerous step for a woman ; and Harriet Martineau had reason for saying at last : " Thus, I am not only entirely satisfied with my lot, but think it the very best for me."

For a while, however, the happy prospect of a beloved wifehood cheered her struggling and anxious life. But it was not for long. Her actual and acknowledged engagement lasted, I believe, only a few months. Mr. Worthington had, at this time, but lately completed his course as a Divinity student; and he had been appointed to the joint charge of a very large Unitarian Church at Manchester. Conscientiousness was one of the most marked features of his character, according to his college friend; and Harriet herself declares that she "venerated his moral nature." He had thrown himself into the very heavy pastoral work committed to him with all the devotion of this high characteristic. Moreover, the long doubt and suspense of his love for her, before their engagement, had, doubtless, worked unfavourably upon his nervous system. The end of it was, that he was suddenly seized with a brain fever, in which he became delirious. He was removed to his father's home in Leicestershire, to be nursed; and, in process of time, the fever was subdued. But the mind did not regain its balance. He was still, as she says, "insane"; but from one of her dear and early friends, I hear that "his family did not call it insanity,"—only a feeble and unhinged state, from which recovery might have been expected hopefully.

In this state of things it was thought desirable that the woman he loved should be brought to see him. The beloved presence, his physician believed, might revive old impressions and happy anticipations, and might be the one thing needful to induce a favourable change in his condition. His mother wrote to beg Harriet Martineau to go to him; Harriet eagerly sought her mother's permission to hasten to his side; and Mrs. Martineau forbad her daughter to go. The old habit of obedience to her mother, and the early

implanted ideas of filial duty, were too strong for
Harriet at once to break through them; she did not
defy her mother and go; and in a few more weeks—
terrible weeks of doubt and mental storm they must
have been, between her love and her obedience dragging
her different ways—Worthington died, and left her to
her life of heart-widowhood, darkened by this shadow
of arbitrary separation to the last.

".The calamity was aggravated to me," she says,
" by the unaccountable insults I received from his
family, whom I had never seen. Years after, the
mystery was explained. They had been given to understand, by cautious insinuations, that I was actually
engaged to another while receiving my friend's addresses." They had not appreciated how submissive
she was as a daughter; and their belief that her love
was insincere was not an unnatural one in the circumstances.

Had those relatives of the dead lover lived to read
Harriet Martineau's Autobiography, they would not
have been made to think differently of her feelings
towards him ; for there she goes calmly on, after the
passage above quoted, to say only : " Considering what
I was in those days, it was happiest for us both that
our union was prevented." As we have had to look
outside the Autobiography for a record of what love
was to her, and what it did for her, so we must seek
elsewhere for the cry of agony which tells how she
felt her loss. But the record exists ; it is found in an
Essay entitled *In a Death Chamber,* one of that
autobiographical series published in *The Monthly
Repository,* from which I have previously quoted.

This beautiful piece of writing—far more of a poem
in essence than anything which she ever published in

verse—is spoiled as a composition by mutilation in quoting. But its length leaves me no option but to select from it only a few of the more confessional passages, to aid us in our psychological study :

This weary watch! In watching by the couch of another there is no weariness ; but this lonely tending of one's own sick heart is more than the worn-out spirit can bear. What an age of woe since the midnight clock gave warning that my first day of loneliness was beginning—to others a Sabbath, to me a day of expiation !

All is dull, cold, and dreary before me, until I also can escape to tho region where there is no bereavement, no blasting root and branch, no rending of the heart-strings. What is aught to me, in the midst of this all-pervading thrilling torture, when all I want is to be dead ? The future is loathsome, and I will not look upon it ; the past, too, which it breaks my heart to think about—what has it been ? It might have been happy, if there is such a thing as happiness ; but I myself embittered it at the time, and for ever. What a folly has mine been ! Multitudes of sins now rise up in the shape of besetting griefs. Looks of rebuke from those now in the grave ; thoughts which they would have rebuked if they had known them ; moments of anger, of coldness ; sympathy withheld when looked for; repression of its signs through selfish pride ; and worse, far worse even than this . . . all comes over me now. O! if there be pity, if there be pardon, let it come in the form of insensibility ; for these long echoes of condemnation will make me desperate.

But was there ever human love unwithered by crime—by crime of which no human law takes cognisance, but the unwritten ever-lasting laws of the affections ? Many will call me thus innocent. The departed breathed out thanks and blessing, and I felt them not then as reproaches. If, indeed, I am only as others, shame, shame on the impurity of human affections; or rather, alas ! for the infirmity of the human heart! For I know not that I could love more than I have loved.

Since the love itself is wrecked, let me gather up its relics, and guard them more tenderly, more steadily, more gratefully. This seems to open up glimpses of peace. O grant me power to retain them—the light and music of emotion, the flow of domestic wisdom and chastened mirth, the life-long watchfulness of benevolence, the thousand thoughts—are these gone in their reality ? Must I forget them as others forget ?

If I were to see *my* departed one—that insensible, wasted form

—standing before me as it was wont to stand, with whom would I exchange my joy? . . . But it is not possible to lose all. The shadows of the past may have as great power as their substance ever had, and the spirit of human love may ever be nigh, invested with a majesty worthy to succeed the lustre of its mortal days.

This is the poem of Harriet Martineau's love. This is what remains to show that the girl whose intellect was so powerful, and who had habitually and of choice exercised her mind upon the most abstruse studies and the most difficult thoughts which can engage the attention, could nevertheless feel at least as fervently, and deliver herself up to her emotions at least as fully, as any feeble, ignorant, or narrow-minded creature that ever lived. Surely with the truth emphasised by such an example, the common but stupid delusion that the development of the intellect diminishes the capacity for passion and tenderness must fade away! This girl's mental power and her mental culture were both un-usually large; but here is the core of her heart, and is it not verily womanly?

This experience did more than give her hours of happiness; it did more than bring to her that enlarge-ment of the spirit which she so well described; for it taught her to appreciate, and to properly value, the influence of the emotions in life. Never in one of her works, never in a single phrase, is she found guilty of that blasphemy against the individual affections, into which some who have yet sought to pose as high priests of the religion of humanity have fallen and lost them-selves. In all her writings one finds the continual recognition of the great truth which was in the mind of him who said: "If a man love not his brother whom he hath seen, how shall he love God whom he hath not seen?"—a truth of the very first consequence to those

who aim at expressing their religion by service to the
progress of mankind.

The year 1826, to Harriet crowded so full of trouble,
came to an end soon after Mr. Worthington's death.
In the following year, though she was in very bad
health, she wrote a vast quantity of manuscript. Some
of it was published at once. Other portions waited in
her desk for a couple of years, when her contributions
to *The Monthly Repository* recommenced, after a
change in its editorship.

She wrote in the year 1827 various short stories,
which were published by Houlston, of Shrewsbury,
without her name on their title-pages. Their character
may be guessed by the fact that they were circulated
as Mrs. Sherwood's writings ! In tone, they resemble
the ordinary Sunday-school story-book ; but there is a
fire, an earnestness, and an originality often discoverable in them which are enough to mark them out from
common hack-writing. Two of them, *The Rioters*
and *The Turn-Out,* deal with topics of political
economy; but the questions were thought out (very
accurately) in her own mind, for at that time she had
never read a book upon the subject.

These little stories were so successful that the publisher invited her to write a longer one, which should
have her name attached to it. She went to work,
accordingly, and produced a good little tale, of one
hundred and fifty pages of print, which she called
*Principle and Practice.* It recounts the struggles of
an orphan family in their efforts after independence.
As in all her writings of this kind, her own experience
is interfused into the fiction. No part of this story is
so interesting as that where a young man who has met
with an accident has to reconcile his mind to the

anticipation of life-long lameness—as she to deafness. The sisters of this orphan family, too, make money by a kind of fancy-work by which she herself was earning a few guineas from the wealthier members of her family, namely, by cutting bags and baskets out of pasteboard, fitting them together with silk and gold braid, and painting plaques upon their sides. *Principle and Practice* was so warmly received in the circle to which it was suited that the publisher called for a sequel, which was accordingly written early in the following year.

There was a vast quantity of writing in all these publications; and, besides this, she was continually at work with her needle. Such unremitting sedentary occupation, together with her sorrow, caused a serious illness, from which she suffered during 1828. It was an affection of the liver and stomach, for which she went to be treated by her brother-in-law, Mr. Greenhow, a surgeon at Newcastle-on-Tyne.

Her remarkable powers of steady application, and her untiring industry, were always* amongst her most noteworthy characteristics—as, indeed, is proved by the vast quantity of work she achieved. In each of her various illnesses, friends who had watched with wonder and alarm how much she wrote, and how unceasingly she worked, either with pen, or book, or needle in hand, told her that her suffering was caused by her merciless industry. Her "staying power" was great; she rarely felt utterly exhausted, and therefore

* "I should think there never was such an industrious lady," said the maid who was with her for the last eleven years of her life; "when I caught sight of her, just once, leaning back in her chair, with her arms hanging down, and looking as though she wasn't even thinking about anything, it gave me quite a turn. I felt she *must* be ill to sit like that!"

she was impatient of being told that she had, in fact, over-exerted her strength. Sometimes, indeed, she admitted that she worked too much, and pleaded only that she could not help it—that the work needed doing, or that the thoughts pressed for utterance, and she could not refuse the call of duty. But more often she said, as in a letter to Mr. Atkinson, which lies before me, " My best aid and support in the miseries of my life has been in *work*—in the intellectual labour which I believe has done me nothing but good." So her immense industry in 1827 may have seemed to her a relief from her heart-sorrows at the moment; but none the less it probably was the chief cause of her partial breakdown in the next year. A blister relieves internal inflammation; but a succession of such stimuli too long continued will exhaust the strength, and render the condition more critical than it would have been without such treatment.

At Newcastle there was a brief cessation from work, under the doctor's orders. But in the middle of 1828 Harriet began to write again for the *Repository,* in response to an appeal put forth by the editor for gratuitous literary aid. That editor was the well-known Unitarian preacher, William Johnston Fox, of South Place Chapel. Mr. Fox became Harriet Martineau's first literary friend. He had no money with which to reward her work for his magazine; but he paid her amply in a course of frank, full, and generous private criticism and encouragement. " His correspondence with me," she says, " was unquestionably the occasion, and, in great measure, the cause, of the greatest intellectual progress I ever made before the age of thirty." Mr. Fox was so acute a critic that he ere long predicted that " she would be one of the first authors of the age if she continued to write "; while, at the same time, he offered suggestions for improvement, and made corrections in her work upon occasion. Her advance in literary capacity was now very rapid. Her style went on improving, as it should do, till her latest years; but it now first became an *individual* one, easy, flowing, forcible, and often most moving and eloquent.

During the latter half of 1828 and the early part of the succeeding year, she contributed, more or less, to nearly every monthly number of the *Repository*, without receiving any payment. She wrote essays, poems, and so-called reviews, which last, however, were really thoughtful and original papers, suggested by the subject of a new book. Some of these contributions were signed " V "; but others, including all the reviews, were anonymous.

Most of these articles are on philosophical subjects, and are written with the calmness of style suitable to logical and argumentative essays. In the *Repository* for February 1829, and the succeeding month, for instance, there appeared two papers, headed, " On the Agency of Feelings in the Formation of Habits," which are simply an accurate, clear, and forcibly-reasoned statement of the philosophical doctrine of Association, with which that of Necessity is inseparably connected. These were, it has been already observed, the theories by which she was learning both to guide her own action and to see that society is moulded, however unconsciously as regards most of the individuals composing it. A clearer statement of the doctrines, or a more forcible indication of how they can be made to serve as a moral impulse, cannot be imagined. Here is very different work from *Devotional Exercises*, or

*Principle and Practice.* But it brought its author neither fame nor money.

Another piece of work done in 1828, or early in the following year, was a *Life of Howard*, which was written on a positive commission from a member of the Committee of Lord Brougham's "Society for the Diffusion of Useful Knowledge," who promised her thirty pounds for it. The MS. was at first said to be lost at the office; eventually she found that its contents were liberally cribbed by the writer of the *Life* which was published; but she never received a penny of the promised payment. These were her times of stress, and struggle, and suffering, and disappointment, in literature as in ordinary life. Her great success, when at last it did come, was so sudden that her previous work was obscured and pushed out of sight in the blaze of triumph. But these years of labour, unrecognised and almost unrewarded, must not be left out of our view, if we would judge fairly of her character. Courage, resolution, self-reliance, determination to conquer in a field once entered upon, are displayed by her quiet industrious perseverance through those laborious years. Harriet Martineau did not make a sudden and easy rush far up the ladder of fame all at once; her climb, like that of most great men and women, was arduous and slow, and her final success proved not only that she had literary ability, but also the strength of character which could work on while waiting for recognition.

Fresh trouble was yet impending. After Mr. Martineau's death, his son Henry remained a partner in the weaving business which the father had carried on so long; and the incomes (small, but sufficient for a maintenance) of the widow and unmarried daughters had to be paid out of the profits of the factory. Just three years after Mr. Martineau's death, however, in June 1829, the old house became bankrupt, with but small assets. Mrs. Martineau and her daughters were thus deprived suddenly of all means of support.

The whole family met this final blow to their fortunes with calm courage. It was soon settled that the two girls who possessed all their senses should go out to teach; but Harriet could not be set to work in the same way—for pupils could not easily be found who would say their lessons into an ear-trumpet. The husband of the lady brought up by Mrs. Martineau with her youngest daughter tells me that upon this occasion Harriet's mother said to her adopted child, " I have no fear for any of my daughters, except poor Harriet; the others can work, but, with her deafness, I do not know how *she* can ever earn her own bread ! "

The first resource for Harriet was fancy work of different kinds. " I could make shirts and puddings," she declares, " and iron, and mend, and get my bread by my needle, if necessary—as it was necessary, for a few months, before I won a better place and occupation with my pen." During the winter which followed the failure of the old Norwich house, she spent the entire daylight hours poring over fancy-work, by which alone she could with certainty earn money. But she did not lay aside the sterner implement of labour for that bright little bread-winner, the needle. After dark she began a long day's literary labour in her own room.

Every night, I believe, I was writing till two, or even three, in the morning, obeying always the rule of the house of being present at the breakfast-table as the clock struck eight. Many a time I was in such a state of nervous exhaustion and distress that I was obliged to walk to and fro in the room before I could put on paper the last line of a page, or the last half-sentence of an essay or review. Yet was I very happy. The deep-felt sense of progress and expansion was delightful; and so was the exertion of all my faculties; and not least, that of Will to overcome my obstructions, and force my way to that power of public speech of which I believed myself more or less worthy.

She offered the results of this nightly literary toil to a great number of magazine editors and publishers, but without the slightest success. Totally unknown in London society, having no literary friends or connections beyond the editor of the obscure magazine of her sect, her manuscripts were scarcely looked at. Everything that she wrote was returned upon her hands, until she offered it in despair to the *Monthly Repository*, where she was as invariably successful. Her work, when published there, however, brought her not an atom of fame, and only the most trifling pecuniary return. She wrote to Mr. Fox, when she found herself penniless, to tell him that it would be impossible for her to continue to render as much gratuitous service as she had been doing to the *Repository*; but he could only reply that the means at his disposal were very limited, and that the utmost he could offer her was £15 a year, for which she was to write "as much as she thought proper." With this letter he forwarded her a parcel of nine books to review, as a commencement. A considerable portion of the space in his magazine was filled by Miss Martineau for the next two years on these terms.

The essay previously referred to, on the "Agency of Feelings in the Formation of Habits," which appeared in the *Repository* for February and March 1829, was Harriet Martineau's first marked work. It was followed up by a series, commencing in the August of

the same year, of " Essays on the Art of Thinking,"
which were continued in the magazine until December,
when two chapters were given in the one number, in
order, as the editor remarked, that his readers " might
possess entire in one volume this valuable manual of
the Art of Thought."

" V," the writer of these articles, was supposed to
be of the superior sex : in those days, Mr. Fox would
have shown rare courage if he had informed his readers
that they were " receiving valuable instruction" in
how to exercise their ratiocinative faculties from the
pen of a woman. In the Index, I find, the references
run—" V.'s" " Ode to Religious Liberty"; *his* " Last
Tree of the Forest"; *his* " Essays on the Art of
Thinking,' &c. &c.

The " Essays on the Art of Thinking " are nothing
less than an outline of Logic. In substance, they present no great originality ; but they display full internal
evidence that the thoughts presented were the writer's
own, and not merely copied from authority. It is
really no light test of clearness and depth of thought
to write on an abstruse science in lucid, perspicuous
fashion, giving a brief but complete view of all its
parts in their true relations. Only an accurate
thinker, with a mind both capacious and orderly, can
perform such a task. The highest function of the
human mind is, doubtless, that of the discoverer. The
original thinker, he who observes his facts from nature
at first hand, who compares them, and reasons about
them, and combines them, and generalises a principle
from them, is the one whom posterity to all time must
honour and reverence for his additions to the store of
human knowledge. But not far inferior in power, and
equal in immediate usefulness, is the disciple who can

judge the originator's work, and, finding it perfectly in
accordance with facts as known to him, can receive it
into his mind, arrange it in order, deck it with illustration, illuminate it with power of language, and represent it in a form suitable for general comprehension.
There is originality of mind needed for such work;
that which is done, the adaptation of the truths to be
received to the receptive powers of the multitude, is an
original work performed upon the truths, hardly inferior in difficulty and utility to that of him who first
discerns them. This was the class of work which
Harriet Martineau was beginning to do, and to do
well. But there was more than this in her purposes.

As these articles, though vastly inferior in execution
to what she afterwards did, nevertheless show the
essential characteristics of her work, this seems to be
the most favourable opportunity to pause to enquire
what was the special feature of her writings. For,
various though her subjects appear to be, ranging from
the humblest topics, such as the duties of maids-of-all-
work, up to the highest themes of mental and political
philosophy, yet I find one informing idea, one and the
same moving impulse to the pen of the writer, throughout the whole series. Let us see what it was that she
really, though half unconsciously perhaps, kept before
her as her aim

It is obvious at once that her writings are all designed to *teach*. A little closer consideration shows
that what they seek to teach is always *what is right
conduct*. Abstract truth merely as such does not
content her. She seeks its practical concrete application to daily life. Further, not merely has she the
aim of teaching morals, but she invariably makes *facts*
and *reasonings from facts the basis* of her moral teach-

ings.   In other words, she approaches morals from the
scientific instead of the intuitional side ; and to thus
influence conduct is the invariable final object of her
writings.

It would sound simpler to say that she wrote on the
science of morals.   But the term " moral science "
has already been appropriated to a class of writing than
which nothing could, very often, less deserve the name
of science.   The work which Harriet Martineau spent
her whole life in doing, was, however, true work in
moral science.   What she was ever seeking to do was
to find out how men should live from what men and
their surroundings are.   She must be recognised as
one of the first thinkers to uniformly consider practical
morals as derived from reasoned science.

Many of the articles contributed to the *Repository*
were naturally, from the character of the publication,
upon theology.   Much that is noticeable might be culled
from amongst them ; as, indeed, could be inferred from
the fact that an able leader of her religious body allowed her to fill so very large a portion of the pages by
which, under his guidance, the Unitarian public were
instructed.   In all the essays, a distinguishing feature
is the earnestness of the effort put forth to judge the
questions at issue by reason, and not by prejudice.
It is true that the effort often fails.   There comes the
moment at which faith in dogma intervenes, and sub-
merges the pure argument; but none the less do the
spirit of justice and fairness, and the love of truth,
irradiate the whole of these compositions.

Mr. Fox soon asked her if she thought that any of
her ideas could be expressed through the medium
of fiction.   It so happened that the suggestion precisely fell in with a thought that had already occurred

to her that "of all delightful tasks, the most delightful would be to describe, with all possible fidelity, the aspect of the life and land of the Hebrews, at the critical period of the full expectation of the Messiah." She wrote a story which she called *The Hope of the Hebrews*, in which a company of young people, relatives and friends, were shown as undergoing the alternations of doubt and hope about whether this teacher was indeed Messiah, on the first appearance of Jesus in Palestine. The day after this story appeared in the *Repository* Mr. Fox was at an Anniversary Dinner of the sect, where so many persons spoke to him about the tale, that he wrote and generously advised Harriet not to publish any more such stories in his magazine, but to make a book of them. She adopted the suggestion; the little volume was issued with her name, and proved her first decisive success. Not only was it well circulated and highly appreciated in England, but it was translated into French, under high ecclesiastical sanction, and was also immediately reproduced in the United States.

While this book was in the press, she went to stay for a short time in London. Mr. Fox, hearing from her how anxious she was to earn her livelihood by literature, succeeded in obtaining from a printer friend of his an offer for her to do " proof correcting and other drudgery," if she liked to remain in London for the work. This would have given her a small but certain income, and there could be little doubt that, if she stayed in London, she would gradually get into some journalistic employment which would enable her to support herself tolerably well. There were no great hopes in the matter. Mr. Fox told her that " one hundred or one hundred and fifty pounds a year is as much as our most successful writers usually make "—success here meaning, of course, full employment in hackwork. It had not yet occurred, even to Mr. Fox, that she was to be really a successful author. But to do even this drudgery, and to take the poor chance now offered to her, implied that she must make her home in London; and she wrote to inform her mother of this fact.

The same post which carried Harriet's letter to this effect, bore to Mrs. Martineau a second missive, from the relative with whom her daughter was staying, which strongly advised that Harriet should be recalled home, there to pursue the needle-work by which she had proved she could earn money. The good lady had been wont to ask Harriet day by day "how much she would get" for the literary labour upon which she had expended some hours ; and the poor young author's reply not being satisfactory or precise, her hostess looked upon the time spent at the desk as so much wasted. She gave Harriet some pieces of silk, " lilac, blue, and pink," and advised her to keep to making little bags and baskets, which the kind friend generously promised to assist in disposing of for good coin of the realm.

The mother who had stood between her full-grown daughter and the bed of a dying betrothed, now thought herself justified in interposing between the woman of twenty-seven and the work which she desired to undertake for her independence. Mrs. Martineau sent Harriet a stern letter, peremptorily ordering her to return home forthwith. Bitterly disappointed at seeing this chance of independence in the vocation she loved thus snatched away, Harriet's sense of filial duty led her to obey her mother's commands.

She went home, with a heavy heart; and with equal sadness, her little sister of eighteen turned out of home, at the same despotic bidding, to go a-governessing. "My mother received me very tenderly. She had no other idea at the moment than that she had been doing her best for my good."

Harriet did not return to Norwich entirely discouraged. Resolution such as hers was not easily broken down. The British and Foreign Unitarian Association had advertised three prizes for the best essays designed to convert Roman Catholics, Jews, and Mohammedans respectively to Unitarianism. The sum offered for each was but small; ten guineas for the Catholic, fifteen for the Jewish, and twenty for the Mohammedan essays. But it was less the money than interest in the cause, and desire to see if she could succeed in competition with others, that led Harriet to form the intention of trying for *all three* prizes.

She went to work immediately upon the Catholic essay, which was to be adjudicated upon six months earlier than the other two. When it was finished, she paid a schoolboy, who wrote a good hand, a sovereign that she could ill spare, for copying the essay, which was about two-thirds the length of this volume. The essays were to be superscribed, as usual in such competitions, with a motto, and the writer's name and address had to be forwarded in a sealed envelope, with the same motto outside. In September, 1830, she received the gratifying news that the Committee of Adjudication had unanimously awarded this prize to her.

The other two essays were commenced with the spirit induced by this success. One of them was copied out by a poor woman, the other by a schoolmaster. Harriet was careful even to have the two essays written upon different sorts of paper, to do them up in differently shaped packages, and to use separate kinds of wax and seals.

The sequel may be told, with all the freshness of the moment, in a quotation from the *Monthly Repository* for May, 1831. " We were about to review it [*i.e.* the Catholic essay] when the somewhat startling fact transpired of her having carried off the other premiums offered by the Association's Committee for tracts addressed to the Mohammedans and the Jews. We shall not now stop to enquire how it has happened that our ministers would not or could not prevent the honour of championing the cause of pure Christianity against the whole theological world from devolving upon a young lady. However that may be, she has won the honour and well deserves to wear it."

The essays were published by the Unitarian Association. There can be little doubt that, however many ministers may have competed, the Committee did select the best papers offered to their choice. The learning in all is remarkable ; the freedom from sectarian bitterness, from bigotry, and from the insolent assumption of moral and religious superiority, is even more striking, in such proselytising compositions.

While waiting the result of the prize competition, Harriet wrote a long story for young people, which she called *Five Years of Youth*. It is one of the prettiest and most attractive of all her writings of this class. It has a moral object, of course—a somewhat similar one to that of Jane Austin's *Sense and Sensibility* ; but the warning against allowing sensitiveness to pass into sentimentality is here directed to girls just budding into womanhood ; and the punishment for the error is

not a love disappointment, but the diminution of the
power of domestic and social helpfulness.

Harriet's work of this year, 1830, comprised the
doing of much fancy-work for sale, making and mending everything that she herself wore, knitting stockings
even while reading, studying a course of German literature, and writing for the press the following quantity of
literary matter :—*Traditions of Palestine,* a duodecimo
volume of 170 printed pages; *Five Years of Youth,* 264
small octavo pages ; three theological essays, making
a closely printed crown octavo volume of 300 pages ;
and fifty-two articles of various lengths in the twelve
numbers of the *Monthly Repository.*

And now she had touched the highest point of sectarian fame. The chosen expositor to the outer world
of her form of religion, and the writer of its favourite
Sunday School story-book of the hour, she must already
have felt that her industrious, resolute labour through
many years had at last borne some fruit.

But the moment for a wider fame and a greater
usefulness was now at hand. In the autumn of 1827
she had read Mrs. Marcet's *Conversations on Political
Economy,* and had become aware that the subject
which she had thought out for herself, and treated in
her little stories of *The Rioters,* and *The Turn-Out,*
was a recognised science. She followed this up by a
study of Adam Smith, and other economists, and the
idea then occurred to her that it might be possible to
illustrate the whole system of Political Economy by
tales similar in style to those she had already written.
The thought had lain working in her mind for long,
and, in this autumn of 1831, the idea began to
press upon her as a duty.

There were many reasons why it was especially neces-

sary just then that the people should be brought to
think about Social Science. The times were bitter
with the evils arising from unwise laws. None know
better than she did how largely the well-being of mankind depends upon causes which cannot be affected
by laws. It is individual conduct which must make or
mar the prosperity of the nation. But, on the other
hand, laws are potent, both as direct causes of evil
conditions (and in a less degree of good conditions),
and from their educational influence upon the people.
Harriet Martineau felt that she had come to see more
clearly than the masses of her fellow-countrymen
exactly how far the miseries under which English
society groaned were caused directly or indirectly by
mischievous legislative Acts. Moreover, the circumstances of the moment made the imparting of such
knowledge not only possible, but specially opportune.
The Bishops had just thrown out the Reform Bill; but
no person who watched the temper of the time could
doubt that their feeble opposition would be speedily
swept aside, and that self-government was about to be
extended to a new class of the people. Most suitable
was the occasion, then, for offering information to
these upon the science and art of society. Harriet
was right in her judgment when she started her pro-
ject of a series of tales illustrative of Political Economy,
under a "thorough, well-considered, steady conviction
that the work was wanted, was even craved by the
popular mind."

She began to write the first of her stories. The
next business was to find a publisher to share her belief
that the undertaking would be acceptable to the public.
She wrote to one after another of the great London
publishers, receiving instant refusals to undertake the

series from all but two; and even these two, after
giving her a little of that delusive hope which ends by
plunging the mind into deeper despair, joined with
their brethren in declining to have anything to do with
the scheme.

Finally, she went to London to try if personal inter-
views would bring her any better success. She stayed
in the house attached to a brewery (Whitbread's), belonging to a cousin of hers, and situated near the City
Road. Thence, she tramped about through the mud
and sleet of December to the publishers' offices, day
after day for nearly three weeks. The result was always
failure. But though she returned to the house worn-
out and dispirited, her determination that the work
should be done never wavered; and night after night
she sat up till long after the brewery clock struck
twelve, the pen pushing on in her trembling hand,
preparing the first two numbers of the series, to be
ready for publication when the means should be found.

It was the kind friend who had helped her before
who came to the rescue at last, at this crisis. Mr.
W. J. Fox induced his brother, Charles, to make her
proposals for publishing her series.

Mr. Charles Fox took care to offer only such arrangement as should indemnify him from all risk in the
undertaking. He required, first, that five hundred
subscribers should be obtained for the work; and
second, that he, the publisher, should receive about
seventy-five per cent of the possible profits. Hopeless
of anything better, she accepted these hard terms, and
it was arranged that the first number should appear
with February 1832.

The original stipulation as to the time that this
agreement should run was that the engagement should

be terminable by either party at the end of every five numbers. But a few days afterwards, when Harriet called upon Mr. W. J. Fox to show him her circular inviting subscribers for the series, she found that Mr. Charles Fox had decided to say that he would not publish more than two numbers, unless a thousand copies of No. 1 were sold in the first fortnight! This decision had been arrived at chiefly in consequence of a conversation which W. J. Fox had held with James Mill, in which the distinguished political econo-mist had pronounced against the essential point of the scheme—the narrative form—and had advised that, if the young lady must try her hand at Political Economy, she should write it in the orthodox didactic style.

Mr. Fox lived at Dalston. When Harriet left his house, after receiving this unreasonable and dis-couraging ultimatum, she—

set out to walk the four miles and a half to the Brewery. I could not afford to ride more or less; but, weary already, I now felt almost too ill to walk at all. On the road, not far from Shoreditch, I became too giddy to stand without some support; and I leaned over some dirty palings, pretending to look at a cabbage-bed, but saying to myself as I stood with closed eyes, " My book will do yet."

That very night she wrote the long, thoughtful, and collected preface to her work. After she had finished it she sat over the fire in her bedroom, in the deepest depression; she cried, with her feet on the fender, till four o'clock, and then she went to bed, and cried there till six, when she fell asleep. But if any persons suppose that because the feminine temperament finds a relief in tears the fact argues weakness, they will be instructed by hearing that she was up by half-past eight, continuing her work, as firmly resolved as ever that it should be published.

# CHAPTER V.

.THE GREAT SUCCESS.

THE work which had struggled into printed existence
with such extreme difficulty raised its author at a
bound to fame.   Ten days after the publication of the
first number, Charles Fox sent Harriet word that not
only were the fifteen hundred copies which formed the
first edition all sold off, but he had such orders in
hand that he proposed to print another five thousand
at once.   The people had taken up the work instantly.
The press followed, instead of leading the public in
this instance ; but it, too, was enthusiastic in praise,
both of the scheme and the execution of the stories.

More than one publisher who had previously rejected
the series made overtures for it now   Its refusal, as
they saw, had been one of those striking blunders of
which literary history has not a few to tell.   But there
is no occasion to cry out about the stupidity of publishers.   They can judge well how far a work written
on lines already popular will meet the demand of the
market ; but an entirely original idea, or the work of
an original writer, is a mere lottery.   There is no
telling how the public will take it until it has been

tried. Publishers put into a good many such lotteries, and often lose by them; then nothing more is heard of the matter. But the cases where they decline a speculation which afterwards turns out to have been a good one are never forgotten. Still, the fact remains that it was Harriet Martineau alone who saw that the people needed her work, and whose wonderful courage and resolution brought it out for the public to accept.

Her success grew, as an avalanche gains in volume, by its own momentum. Besides the publishers' communications she had letters, and pamphlets, and blue-books, and magazines forwarded to her in piles, in order that she might include the advocacy of the senders' hobbies in her series. One day the postmaster sent her a message that she must let a barrow be fetched for her share of the mail, as it was too bulky to come in any other way. Lord Brougham declared that it made him tear his hair to think that the Society for the Diffusion of Knowledge, which he had instituted for the very purpose of doing such work as she was undertaking, seemed not to have a man in it with as much sense of what was wanted as this little deaf girl at Norwich. The public interest in the work was, perhaps, heightened by the fact that so ignorant was everybody of her personality, that this description of Brougham's passed muster. But she was not little, and she was now twenty-nine years of age.

She stayed in Norwich, going on writing hard, until the November of 1832, by which time eight numbers of her series had appeared. Then she went to London, taking lodgings with an old servant of Mrs. Martineau's, who lived in Conduit Street. In the course of a few months, however, Mrs. Martineau settled herself in London, and her daughter again resided with her, in a house in Fludyer Street, Westminster.

The purely literary success which she had hitherto enjoyed was now turned into a social triumph. However she might strive against being lionised she could not avoid the attentions and honours that were poured upon her. It is little to say that all the distinguished people in town hastened to know her; it was even considered to give distinction to a party if she could be secured to attend it. Literary celebrities, titled people, and members of Parliament, competed for the small space of time that she could spare for society.

This was not very much, for the work she had undertaken was heavy enough to absorb all her energies. She had engaged to produce one of her stories every month. They were issued in small paper-covered volumes of from one hundred and twenty to one hundred and fifty pages of print. She began publication with only two or three numbers ready written. Thus, to keep on with her series, she had to write one whole number every month. It would have been hard work had it been simple story-telling, had she been merely imaginatively reproducing scenes and characters from her past experience, or writing according to her fancy. But it was, in fact, a much more difficult labour upon which she was engaged. Her scheme required that she should embody every shade of variety of the human character; that her scenes should be laid in different parts of the world, with topography and surroundings appropriate to the story; and that the governments and social state of all these various places should be accurately represented. In addition to all this she had to lay down for each tale the propositions which had to be illustrated in it; to assure herself that she

clearly saw the truth and the bearings of every doctrine
of Political Economy; and then to work into a connected fiction in a concrete form the abstract truths
of the science—representing them as exemplified in
the lives of individuals.

Political Economy treats of the production, distribution, and consumption, or use, of all the material objects
of human desire, which are called by the general name
of wealth. Thus, it is a subject which concerns every
one of us in our daily lives, and not merely a matter
belonging (as its name unfortunately leads many to
suppose) entirely to the province of the legislator. The
great mass of mankind are producers of wealth. All
are necessarily consumers—for the bare maintenance of
existence demands the consumption of wealth. The
well-being of the community depends upon the industry and skill with which wealth is produced; upon
the distribution of it in such a manner as to encourage
future production; and upon the consumption of it
with due regard to the claims of the future. It is
individuals who, as the business of common life, produce, exchange, divide, and consume wealth; it is,
therefore, each individual's business to comprehend the
science which treats of his daily life. A science is
nothing but a collection of facts, considered in their
relationship to each other. Miss Martineau's plan, in
her series, was strictly what I have indicated as being
always her aim; namely, to deduce from an abstract
science rules for daily life—the secondary, practical,
or concrete science. It was the union of a scientific
basis with practical morals that made this subject
attractive to her mind, and led her (in the words of
her preface), to " propose to convey the leading truths
of Political Economy, as soundly, as systematically, as

clearly and faithfully, as the utmost painstaking and the strongest attachment to the subject will enable us to do."

She did her work very methodically. Having first noted down her own ideas on the branch of the subject before her, she read over the chapters relating to it in the various standard works that she had at hand, making references as she read. The next thing to do was to draw out as clearly and concisely as possible the truths that she had to illustrate; this " summary of principles," as she called it, was affixed to each tale. By this time she would see in what part of the world, and amongst what class of people, the principles in question were operating most manifestly; and if this consideration dictated the choice of a foreign background, the next thing to be done was to get from a library works of travel and topography, and to glean hints from them for local colouring.

The material thus all before her in sheets of notes, she reduced it to chapters; sketching out the characters of her *dramatis personæ*, their action, and the features of the scenes, and also the Political Economy which they had to convey either by exemplification or by conversation. Finally, she paged her paper. Then " the story went off like a letter. I did it," she says, " as I write letters; never altering the expression as it came fresh from my brain."

I have seen the original manuscript of one of the Political Economy Tales. It shows the statement just quoted to be entirely accurate. The writing has evidently been done as rapidly as the hand could move ; every word that will admit of it is contracted, to save time. " Socy.," "opporty.," "agst.," "abt.," "independce.," these were amongst the abbreviations submitted to

the printer's intelligence; not to mention commoner
and more simple words, such as wh., wd., and the like.
The calligraphy, though very readable, has a somewhat
slipshod look. Thus, there is every token of extremely
rapid composition. Yet the corrections on the MS.
are few and trifling; the structure of a sentence is
never altered, and there are but seldom emendations
even of principal words. The manuscript is written
(in defiance of law and order) on both sides of the
paper; the latter being quarto, of the size now commonly called *sermon* paper, but, in those pre-envelope
ages, it was letter paper.

Her course of life in London was as follows: she
wrote in the morning, rising, and making her own
coffee at seven, and going to work immediately after
breakfast until two. From two till four she saw visitors. Having an immense acquaintance, she declined
undertaking to make morning calls; but people might
call upon her any afternoon. She was charged with
vanity about this arrangement; but, with the work on
her hands and the competition for her company, she
really could not do differently. Still, Sydney Smith
suggested a better plan; he told her she should " hire
a carriage, and engage an inferior authoress to go
round in it to drop the cards!" After any visitors left,
she went out for her daily " duty walk," and returned
to glance over the newspapers, and to dress for dinner.
Almost invariably she dined out, her host's or some other
friend's carriage being commonly sent to fetch her. One
or two evening parties would conclude the day, unless the
literary pressure was extreme, in which case she would
sometimes write letters after returning home. During
the whole time of writing her series, she was satisfied
with from five to six hours sleep out of the twenty-

four; and though she was not a teetotaller, but drank wine at dinner, still she took no sort of stimulant to help her in her work.

This was the course of life that a woman, of no extraordinary physical strength, was able to maintain with but little cessation or interval for two years. When I look at the thirty-four little volumes which she produced in less than as many months, and when I consider the character of their contents, I am bound to say that I consider the feat of mere industry unparalleled, within my knowledge.

The *Illustrations of Political Economy* are plainly and inevitably damaged, as works of art, by the fact that they are written to convey definite lessons. The fetters in which the story moves are necessarily far closer than in the ordinary " novel with a purpose "; for here the object is not merely to show the results, upon particular characters or upon individual careers, of a certain course of conduct, and thence to argue that in similar special circumstances all persons would experience similar consequences : but the task here is to show in operation those springs of the social machinery by which we are *all*, generally quite unconsciously, guided in our *every-day* actions, the natural laws by which *all* our lives are *inevitably* governed. To do this, the author was compelled to select scenes from common life, and to eschew the striking and the unusual. Again, it was absolutely necessary that much of the doctrine which had to be taught must be conveyed by dialogue; not because it would not be possible to exemplify in action every theory of Political Economy— for all those theories have originally been derived from observation of the facts of human history— but because no such a small group of persons and such a limited space of time as must be taken to *tell a story about*, can possibly display the whole consequences of many of the laws of social science. The results of our daily actions as members of society are not so easily visible as they would be if we could wholly trace them out amongst our own acquaintances or in our own careers. The consequences of our own conduct, good or bad, must *come round* to us, it is true, but often only as members of the body politic. Thus, they are very often in a form as little distinguishable to the uninstructed mind as we may suppose it would be comprehensible to the brain, if the organs of the body had a separate con-sciousness, that it was responsible for its own aches arising from the disturbance of the liver consequent upon intemperance. But in a tale it is obviously im-possible to show *in action* any more of the working of events than can be exemplified in one or two groups of persons, all of whom must be, however slightly, personally associated. The larger questions and prin-ciples at issue must be expounded and argued out in conversations, or else by means of an entire lapse from the illustrative to the didactic method. Now, as ordi-nary people do not go about the world holding long conversations or delivering themselves of dissertations on political economy, it is clear that the introduction of such talks and preachments detracts from the excel-lence of the story as a work of art. Still less artis-tically admirable does the fiction become when a lesson is introduced as a separate argument intruded into the course of the tale.

Political Economy as a science was then but fifty years old. Adam Smith had first promulgated its fundamental truths in his immortal *Wealth of Nations*, in 1776. Malthus, Ricardo, and one or two others had since added to the exposition of the facts and the relationship between the facts (that is to say, the science) of social arrangements. But it was not then— nor is it, indeed, yet, in an age when the great rewards of physical research have attracted into that field nearly all the best intellects for science of the time—a complete body of reasoned truths. Some of the positions laid down by all the earlier writers are now discredited; others are questioned. In a few passages, accordingly, these tales teach theories which would now require revision. It must be added at once that these instances are few and far between. The reasoning, the grasp of the facts of social life and the logical acumen with which they are dissected and explained in these tales, are generally speaking nearly perfect, and therefore such as all competent students of the subject would at this day endorse. The slips in exposition of the science as it was then understood are *exceedingly* rare. Greater clearness, and more precision, and better arrangement, could hardly have been attained had years been spent upon the work, in revising, correcting, and re-copying, instead of each "Illustration" being written in a month, and sent to press with hardly a phrase amended.

The accuracy and excellence in the presentation of the science were admitted at once by the highest authorities. Mr. James Mill early made honourable amends for his previous doubts as to the possibility of Miss Martineau's success. Whately and Malthus expressed their admiration of the work. Lord Brougham called upon her, and engaged her pen to illustrate the necessity for reform in the treatment of the social canker of pauperism. The Gurneys, and the rest of the Quaker Members of Parliament, got Mrs. Fry to make an appointment to ask Miss Martineau's advice as to their action in the House on the same subject, when it was ripe for legislation. The Chancellor of the Exchequer (Lord Althorp) even sent his private secretary (Mr. Drummond, the author of the world-famous phrase "Property has its duties as well as its rights") to supply Miss Martineau with information to enable her to prepare the public for the forthcoming Budget. The Chairman of the Royal Commission on Excise Taxes gave her the manuscript of the evidence taken, and the draft of the report of the Commission, before they were formally presented to the Ministers of the Crown (a thing without precedent!), in order that she might use the facts to pave the way for the reception of the report in the House and by the people. The whole public of male students of her science paid her work what men consider in their unconscious insolence to be the highest compliment that they *can* pay a woman's work : the milder-mannered ones said she had "a masculine intelligence"; the stronger characters went further, and declared that the books were so good that it was impossible to believe them to be written by a woman. Newspaper critics not infrequently attributed them to Lord Brougham, then Lord Chancellor ; that versatile and (at the moment) most popular politician was supposed either to write them all himself, or to supply their main features for the inferior mind to throw into shape.

While statesmen, politicians, thinkers, and students were thus praising the clearness and appreciating the power of the work as political economy, the general public eagerly bought and read the books, both for their bearing on the legislative questions of the day and for their vividness and interest as stories. And indeed, they richly deserved to be read as works of fiction. Remembering the limitations to their artistic excellence previously adverted to, they may be with justice praised for most of the essential features of good novel-writing.

The characters are the strongest point. Clearly individualised, consistently carried out, thinking, speaking, and acting in accordance with their nature, the characters are always personages; and some of them must live long in the memories of those who have made their acquaintance. The sterner virtues in Cousin Marshall, in Lady F——, in Ella of Garveloch, and in Mary Kay, are no less clearly and attractively depicted than the milder and more passive ones in the patience of Christian Vanderput, in the unconscious devotion to duty of Nicholas, in the industry and hopefulness of Frank and Ellen Castle, in the wifely love and agony of Hester Morrison, in the quiet public spirit of Charles Guyon, in the proved patriotism of the Polish exiles, and in a dozen other instances. Her feelings and her spirit are at home in depicting these virtues of the character; but none the less does she well succeed in realising both vice and folly. Her real insight into character was quite remarkable; as Dr. Martineau observed to me, when he said, " My sister's powers of observation were extraordinary." If, on the one hand, her deafness often prevented her from appreciating the delicacies and the chances of verbal expression (which really reveal so much of the nature) in those around her, so that she was apt to draw sharper lines than most people do between the sheep and the goats in her estimation; on the other hand, she saw, more than those whose minds are distracted by sounds, the light and play of the countenance, and the indications of character in trivial actions. The excellence of her character-drawing in these novels gives abundant evidence that the disqualification was more than counterbalanced by the cultivation of the other faculty.

The unconsciousness of her mental analysis is at once its greatest charm and the best token of its truthfulness. Florence Nightingale realised how fully this was so with reference to the finer qualities of morals. In her tribute to Harriet Martineau's memory Miss Nightingale justly observes :—

In many parts of her *Illustrations of Political Economy*—for example, the death of a poor drinking-woman, " Mrs. Kay,"—what higher religious feeling (or *one should rather say instinct*) could there be ? To the last she had religious feeling—in the sense of good working out of evil into a supreme wisdom penetrating and moulding the whole universe ; into the natural subordination of intellect and intellectual purposes and of intellectual self to purposes of good, even were these merely the small purposes of social or domestic life.

On the other side of the human character, in her delineation of the bad qualities, she as instinctively seeks and finds causes for the errors and evils of the minds she displays. Foolishness, and ignorance, and poverty are traced, entirely without affectation and " cant," in their action as misleading influences in the lives of the poor sinners and sufferers.

The stories told in the *Illustrations* are frequently very interesting. In this respect, there is a notable advance in the course of the series. The earlier tales, such as *Life in the Wilds* and *Brooke Farm*, are not to be compared as mere stories with even those written later on by only eight or nine stirring eventful months, such as *Ireland*, and *The Loom and the Lugger*. Still better are the latest tales. The *Illustrations of Taxation*, and *Illustrations of Poor-Laws aad Paupers* are, despite the unattractiveness of their topics, of the highest interest. *The Parish, The Town, The Jerseymen Meeting, The Jerseymen Parting,* and *The Scholars of Arnside,* would assuredly be eagerly read by any lover of fiction, almost without consciousness that there was anything in the pages except a deeply interesting story.

Archbishop Whately pronounced *The Parish* the best thing she had done. *Vanderput and Snook,* the story dealing with bills of exchange, was the favourite with Mr. Hallam. Lord Brougham, on whose engagement she did the five "Poor-Law" stories, wrote most enthusiastically that they surpassed all the expectations that her previous works had led him to form. Coleridge told her that he "looked eagerly every month" for the new number; and Lord Durham recounted to her how one evening he was at Kensington Palace (where the widowed Duchess of Kent was then residing, and devoting herself to that education which has made her daughter the best sovereign of her dynasty), when the little Princess Victoria came running from an inner room to show her mother, with delight, the advertisement of the "Taxation" tales; for the young Princess was being allowed to read the *Illustrations,* and found them her most fascinating story-books.

Harriet's experiences, however, were not all quite so agreeable. Mrs. Marcet, who "had a great opinion of great people—of people great by any distinction, ability, office, birth and what not—and innocently supposed her own taste to be universal," formed a warm and generous friendship for Miss Martineau, and used to delight in carrying to her the "homages" of the savants and the aristocratic readers of the *Illus-*

*trations* in France, where Mrs. Marcet's acquaintance
was extensive. She one day told Miss Martineau,
with much delight, that Louis Philippe, the then King
of the French, had ordered a copy of the series for each
member of his family, and had also requested M.
Guizot to have the stories translated, and introduced
into the French national schools. This was presently
confirmed by a large order from France for copies,
and by a note from the officially-appointed translator
requesting Harriet Martineau to favour him with some
particulars of her personal history, for introduction
into a periodical which was being issued by the Government for the promotion of education amongst the
French people. The writer added that M. Guizot
wished to have Miss Martineau's series specially noticed
in connection with her own personality, since she
afforded the first instance on record of a woman who
was not born to sovereign station affecting practical
legislation otherwise than through a man.

At the very time that she received this flattering
note, Harriet was engaged in writing her twelfth
number, *French Wines and Politics.* The topic treated
in this story is that of value, with the subsidiary questions relating to prices and their fluctuations. The
tale takes up the period of the great French Revolution, and shows how the fortunes of certain wine-
merchants near Bordeaux, and of the head of the Paris
house in connection, were affected by the course of that
great social convulsion. The scene was unquestionably
happily chosen. The circumstances were abnormal,
it is true; but the causes which created such vast
fluctuations in prices, and such changes in the
value of goods, were, in fact, only the same fundamental causes as are always at the basis of such

alterations in price and value; it was merely the rapidity and violence of the movement which were peculiar. The story was well put together; and the " Illustration" was in every way admirable for every possibly desirable object, except only for the one of being pleasant to the ruling powers in the France of 1833.

Harriet Martineau's constant sympathy with democracy, her hatred of oppression and tyranny, and her aversion to class government, all became conspicuous in this story. " The greatest happiness of the greatest number " of mankind was her ideal of the aim of legislation; and she well knew, as Bentham saw, that only the democratic form of Government can produce a body of laws approximating to this ideal. Her efforts were constant, therefore, to prepare the people to demand, and to afterwards wisely use, the power of governing themselves. Now, though Louis Philippe was the citizen-king, though he was the head of a Republican Monarchy, though his legislative chamber rejected in that same year a ministerial document because it spoke of the people as " subjects," yet it may be easily understood that this king and his ministers did not care to stimulate the democratic feeling of the nation any more than they found inevitable. The whole tone of this work would be objectionable to them; and a dozen passages might be readily quoted to show why royal and aristocratic rulers were little likely to aid its circulation amongst the people whom they governed. Here, for instance, is a portion of the passage on the storming of the Bastille:—

The spectacles of a life-time were indeed to be beheld within the compass of this one scene. . . . Here were the terrors which sooner or later chill the marrow of despotism, and the stern joy

with which its retribution fires the heart of the patriot.  Here
were the servants of tyranny quailing before the glance of the
people. . . . The towers of palaces might be seen afar, where
princes were quaking at this final assurance of the downfall of
their despotic sway, knowing that the assumed sanctity of royalty
was being wafted away with every puff of smoke which spread
itself over the sky, and their irresponsibility melting in fires lighted
by the hands which they had vainly attempted to fetter, and blown
by the breath which they had imagined they could stifle.  They
hád denied the birth of that liberty whose baptism in fire and in
blood was now being celebrated in a many-voiced chaunt with
which the earth should ring for centuries.  Some from other lands
were already present to hear and join in it; some free Britons to
aid, some wondering slaves of other despots to slink homewards
with whispered tidings of its import; for from that day to this, the
history of the fall of the Bastille has been told as a secret in the
vineyards of Portugal, and among the groves of Spain, and in
the patriotic conclaves of the youth of Italy, while it has been
loudly and joyfully proclaimed from one end to the other of Great
Britain, till her lisping children are familiar with the tale.

Besides such passages as this, scarcely likely to please
the French king, there was the special ground for his
objection that his immediate ancestor, Egalité, was introduced into the story, and depicted in no favourable
light—his efforts to inflame the popular violence for his
selfish ends, his hypocrisy, his cowardice, and so on,
being held up to contempt.  Mrs. Marcet, when she
read all this, came breathless to Harriet Martineau to
ask her how she could have made such a blunder as
to write a story that plainly would (and, of course, in
fact, did) put an end to the official patronage of her
series in France, and would destroy for ever any hopes
that she might have entertained of being received at
the Court of Louis Philippe?  Greatly surprised was
the good lady at finding Harriet's reverence for that
monarch so limited in extent.  She replied to her kind
friend that she " wrote with a view to the people, and
especially the most suffering of them ; and the crowned

heads must for once take their chance for their feelings."

At the very moment that Mrs. Marcet's remonstrance
was made, Miss Martineau was writing a story of a
character likely to be even more distasteful to the
Emperor of Russia than this one to the King of
the French. She had found it difficult to illustrate the
theory of the currency in a story treating of the existence of civilised people. The only situation in which
she could find persons, above the rank of savages,
transacting their exchanges by aid of a kind of money
which made the business only one remove from barter-
ing, was amongst the Polish exiles in Siberia. She therefore wrote *The Charmed Sea,* a story founded upon the
terrible facts of the lives of the exiled Poles " in the
depths of Eastern Siberia," working in " a silver-mine
near the western extremity of the Daourian Range,
and within hearing of the waters of the Baikal when
its storms were fiercest." Had the melancholy tale
been written in the service of the Poles, it could not
have been more moving. So powerful and interesting
was it, indeed, that the criticism of the *Edinburgh Review*
was that the fiction too entirely overpowered the political economy. The arrival of *The Charmed Sea* in
Russia changed the favourable opinion which the
Czar had previously been so kind as to express about
the *Illustrations,* He had been purchasing largely of the
French translation of the series for distribution amongst
his people. But now he issued a proclamation ordering every copy in Russia of every number to be immediately burnt, and forbidding the author ever to set foot
upon his soil. Austria, equally concerned in the Polish
business, followed this example, and a description of
Harriet Martineau's person was hung in the appointed

places, amidst the lists of the proscribed, all over Russia, Austria, and Austrian-Italy. Despots, at least, had no admiration for her politics.

The only important adverse criticism in the press appeared in the *Quarterly Review.*\* The reviewer objected impartially to every one of the twelve stories which had then appeared. Every circumstance which could arouse prejudice against the series was taken advantage of, from party political feeling and religious bigotry, down to the weakness of fluid philanthropy, and " the prudery and timidity of the middle-classes of England." The principal ground of attack was the story which dealt with Malthusianism, *Weal and Woe in Garveloch.*

When the course of my exposition brought me to the population subject, I, with my youthful and provincial mode of thought and feeling—brought up, too, amidst the prudery which is found in its great force in our middle class—could not but be sensible that I risked much in writing and publishing on a subject which was not universally treated in the pure, benevolent, and scientific spirit of Malthus himself. . . . I said nothing to anybody; and, when the number was finished, I read it aloud to my mother and aunt. If there had been any opening whatever for doubt or dread, I was sure that these two ladies would have given me abundant warning and exhortation—both from their very keen sense of propriety and their anxious affection for me. But they were as complacent and easy as they had been interested and attentive. I saw that all ought to be safe.

The *Quarterly Review* seized the opportunity of the appearance of this number to make a vile attack upon the series and its writer. Harriet suffered under it to a degree which seems almost excessive. The review

---

\* In the same number, by the way, appeared the notorious biting and sarcastic notice of Tennyson's second volume. It is a distinction, indeed, for a critical review, that one number should have devoted half its space to violently unfavourable criticisms of Alfred Tennyson's poetry and Harriet Martineau's political economy.

is so obviously full of fallacies, as regards its Political Economy, that any person whose opinion was worth having could hardly hesitate in deciding that she, and not her critic, was talking common-sense and arguing logically. As to the personal part of the article, it is, though scurrilous, and even indecent, so very funny that the attacked might almost have forgotten the insult in the amusement. Nevertheless, the writers, Croker and Lockhart, did their worst. Croker openly said that he expected to lose his pension very shortly, and, being wishful to make himself a literary position before that event happened, he had begun by "toma-hawking Miss Martineau." All that could be painful to her as a woman, and injurious to her as a writer, was said, or attempted to be conveyed, in this article.

Let us see what it was all about. Garveloch, one of the Hebridean islands, is seen in the " Illustration " rapidly multiplying its population, both by early mar-riages and by immigration, under the stimulus of a passing prosperity in the fishing industry. The influx of capital and the increase of the demand for food, have led to such an improvement in the cultivation of the land, that the food produce of the island has been doubled in ten years. Ella, the heroine (a fine, strong, self-contained, helpful woman—one of the noblest female characters in these works), foresees that if the reckless increase of population continues, the supply of food will by-and-bye run short. Her interlocutor asks how this will be the case, since the population will surely not double again, as it has done already, in ten years? Then the *Quarterly* quotes Ella's reply, and comments on it:—

"Certainly not; but say twenty, thirty, fifty, or any number of years you choose; still, as the number of the people doubles itself

for ever, while the produce of the land does not, the people must
increase faster than the produce."

This is rare logic and arithmetic, and not a little curious as
natural history. A plain person, now, would have supposed that if
the produce doubled itself in ten, and the people only in a hundred
years, the people would not increase *quite* so fast as the produce,
seeing that at the end of the first century the population would be
multiplied but by two, the produce by one thousand and twenty-
four. But these are the discoveries of genius! Why does Miss
Martineau write, except to correct our mistaken notions and
expound to us the mysteries of "the principle of population."

The reviewer goes on to suggest, in the broadest
language, that she has confounded the rate of the
multiplication of the herring-fisherwomen with that
of the herrings themselves; reproves her for writing
on "these ticklish topics" with so little physiological information; and tells her that she, "poor
innocent, has been puzzling over Mr. Malthus's arith-
metical and geometrical ratios for knowledge which
she should have obtained by a simple question or two
of her mamma." In one and the same paragraph, he
tells her that he is "loth to bring a blush unnecessarily
upon the cheek of any woman," and asks her if she
picked up her information on the subject "in her
conferences with the Lord Chancellor?"

This is enough to show to what a sensitive young
lady was exposed in illustrating "a principle as unde-
niable as the multiplication table," and in stating the
facts upon which hangs the explanation of the poverty,
and therefore of a large part of the vice and misery,
of mankind. Miss Martineau's exposition was, of
course, entirely right, and the fallacy in the review
is obvious, one would suppose, on the surface. The
reviewer's error consists in his assumption—the falsity
of which is at once apparent on the face of the
statement—that land can go on doubling its produce

*every* ten years, for an indefinite period.  So far from this being true, the fact is that the limit of improving the cultivation of land is soon reached.  Better agricultural treatment may easily make half-cultivated land bring forth double its previous produce ; but the highest pitch of farming once reached—as it comparatively soon is—the produce cannot be further increased ; and even before this limit is reached, the return for each additional application of capital and labour becomes less and less proportionately bountiful. This is the truth known to political economists as "the Law of the diminishing Return of Land." Taken in conjunction with the fact that the human race *can* double for ever, theoretically, and in reality *does* multiply its numbers with each generation, checked only by the forethought of the more prudent and the operation of famine, war, crime, and the diseases caused by poverty, this law explains why mankind does not more rapidly improve its condition—why the poor have been always with us—and why teaching such as Harriet Martineau here gave must be received into the popular mind before the condition of society can be expected to be improved in the only way possible, by the wisdom and prudence of its members.

Painful as was the attack she had undergone, intensely as she had suffered from its character and nature, Miss Martineau did not allow what she had felt of personal distress to have any influence on her future writings.  Her moral courage had been well trained and exercised, first by the efforts that her mind had had to make in following her conscience as a guide to the formation of opinions, in opposition to the tendency implanted by her mother's treatment to bow supinely before authority; secondly, by the

lesson of endurance which her deafness had brought
to her.   She had now to show, for the first, but by no
means the last time, that hers was one of those tem-
peraments which belong to all leaders of men, whether
in physical or moral warfare; that danger was to her
a stimulus, and that her courage rose the higher the
greater the demand for its exercise.

Praise and blame, appreciation and defamation,
strengthened and enlarged her mind during this period.
But at the end of it, Sydney Smith could say : " She
has gone through such a season as no girl before ever
knew, and she has kept her own mind. her own
manners, and her own voice.   She 's safe.'

# CHAPTER VI.

On the conclusion of the publication of the *Illustrations of Political Economy,* Harriet went to the United States, and travelled there for more than two years. Her fame had preceded her; and she received the warm and gracious greeting from the generous people of America that they are ever ready to give to distinguished guests from their " little Mother-isle." She travelled not only in the Northern States, but in the South and the West too, going in the one direction from New York to New Orleans, and in the other to Chicago and Michigan. Everywhere she was received with eager hospitality. Public institutions were freely thrown open to her, and eminent citizens vied with each other in showing her attention, publicly and privately.

The most noteworthy incident in the course of the whole two years was her public declaration of her anti-slavery principles. The Anti-Slavery movement was in its beginning. The Abolitionists were the subjects of abuse and social persecution, and Miss Martineau was quickly made aware that by a declaration in their

favour she would risk incurring odium, and might
change her popularity in society into disrepute and
avoidance.   It would have been perfectly easy for a
less active conscience and a less true moral sense
to have evaded the question, in such a manner that
neither party could have upbraided her for her action.
She might simply have said that she was there as a
learner, not as a teacher; that her business was to
survey American society, and not to take any share in
its party disputes, or to give any opinion on the political questions of a strange land.   Such paltering with
principle was impossible to Harriet Martineau.   She
did not obtrude her utterances on the subject, but when
asked in private society what she thought, she frankly
spoke out her utter abhorrence, not merely of slavery
in the abstract, but also of the state of the Southern
slave-holders and their human property.   She could
not help seeing that this candour often gave offence ;
but that was not her business when her opinion was
sought on a moral question.

The really searching test of her personal character
did not come, however, with regard to this matter,
till she went to stay for a while in Boston, the head-
quarters of the Abolitionists, fifteen months after her
arrival in America.   It happened that she reached
Boston the very day a ladies' anti-slavery meeting was
broken up by the violence of a mob, and that Garrison,
falling into the hands of the enraged multitude, was
half-murdered in the street.   Harriet had given a
promise, long previously, to attend an Abolitionists'
meeting ; and though these occurrences showed her that
there was actual personal danger in keeping her word,
she was not to be intimidated.   She went to the very
next meeting of the ladies' society, which was held a

month after the one so violently disturbed, and there, being unexpectedly begged to "give them the comfort" of a few words from her, she rose, and, as the official report says, "with great dignity and simplicity of manner," declared her full sympathy with the principles of the association.

She knew well how grave would be the social consequences to her of thus throwing in her lot with the despised and insulted Abolitionists; but she felt that she "could never be happy again" if she shrank from the duty of expression thrust upon her. The results to her were as serious as she had apprehended. She received innumerable personal insults and slights, public and private, where before all had been homage; the Southern newspapers threatened her personal safety, calling her a "foreign incendiary"; and, to crown all, she had to give up an intended Ohio tour, on the information of an eminent Cincinnati merchant that he had heard with his own ears the details of a plot to hang her on the wharf at Louisville, before the respectable inhabitants could intervene, in order to " warn all other meddlesome foreigners."

All this abuse and insult and threatening from the lower kind of persons, interested for their purses, had, of course, no influence upon the hundred private friendships that she had formed. Ardent and deep was the affection with which many Americans came to regard her, and with some of them her intimate friendship lasted through all the succeeding forty years of her life. Emerson was one of these friends, and Garrison another. It was her frequent correspondence with these and many others that kept her interest in the affairs of the United States so active, and made her so well-informed about them as to give her the great authority that she had, both in England and America, during the life and death struggle of the Union, so that at that time, when she was writing leaders for the London *Daily News,* Mr. W. E. Forster said that " it was Harriet Martineau alone who was keeping English public opinion about America on the right side through the press."

Loth to leave such friendships behind, and yet longing for home, she sailed from New York at the end of July 1836, and reached Liverpool on the 26th August. A parting act of American chivalry was that her ship-passage was paid for her by some unknown friend.

It was while she was in the United States that the first portrait of her which I have seen was painted. She herself did not like it, calling the attitude melo-dramatic ; but her sister Rachael, I am told, always declared that it was the only true portrait of Harriet that was ever taken. At this point, then, some idea of her person may be given.

She was somewhat above the middle height, and at this time had a slender figure. The face in the por-trait is oval ; the forehead rather broad, as well as high, but not either to a remarkable degree. The most noticeable peculiarity of the face is found in a slight projection of the under lip. The nose is straight, not at all turned up at the end, but yet with a definite tip to it. The eyes are a clear grey, with a calm, stead-fast, yet sweet gaze ; indeed, there is an almost appealing look in them. The hair is of so dark a brown as to appear nearly black. A tress of it (cut off twenty years later than this American visit, when it had turned snow-white) has been given to me ; and I find the treasured relic to be of exceptionally fine texture—a sure sign of a delicate and sensitive nervous organization. Her hands and feet were small.

She was certainly not beautiful; besides the slight projection of the lower lip the face has the defect of the cheeks sloping in too much towards the chin. But she was not strikingly plain either. The countenance in this picture has a look both of appealing sweetness and of strength in reserve; and one feels that with such beauty of expression it could not fail to be attractive to those who looked upon it with sympathy.

The competition amongst the publishers for Miss Martineau's book on America was an amusing contrast to the scorn with which her proposals for her *Political Economy* had been received. Murray sent a message through a friend, offering to undertake the American work; and letters from two other publishers were awaiting her arrival in England. On the day that the newspapers announced that she had reached town no fewer than three of the chief London publishers called upon her with proposals. She declined those of Bentley and Colburn, and accepted the offer of Messrs. Saunders and Otley to pay her £300 per volume for the first edition of three thousand copies. The book appeared in three volumes, so that she received £900 for it. She completed the three goodly volumes in six months.

She had wished to call the book *Theory and Practice of Society in America*, a title which would have exactly expressed the position that she took up in it, viz. that the Americans should be judged by the degree in which they approached, in their daily lives, to the standard of the principles laid down in their Constitution. Her publishers so strongly objected to this title, that she

consented to call the work simply *Society in America.*
She held to her scheme none the less, and the book
proceeds upon it.   She quotes the Declaration of Independence that all men are created equal, with an
inalienable right to life, liberty, and the pursuit of happiness, and that Governments derive their just powers
from the consent of the governed.   " Every true citizen,"
she claims, " must necessarily be content to have his
self-government tried by the test of the principles to
which, by his citizenship, he has become a subscriber."
She brings social life in the United States of 1834–6
to this test accordingly.

That method of approaching her subject had some
advantages.   It enabled her to treat with peculiar
force the topics of slavery, of the exclusion of women
from political affairs, and of the subservience to the
despotism of public opinion which she found to exist
at that time in America.

But she herself came to see, in after times, that her
*plan* (leaving the details aside) was radically faulty.
She was, as she says, " at the most metaphysical
period " of her mental history.   Thus, she failed at
the moment to perceive that she commenced her subject
*at the wrong end* in taking a theory and judging the
facts of American society by their agreement or dis-
agreement with that *à priori* philosophy.   It was the
theory that had to be judged by the way in which the
people lived under a government framed upon it, and
not the people by the degree in which they lived up
to the theory.   The English public wanted a book that
would help them to know the American public and
its ways ; the Americans required to see through the
eyes of an observant, cultivated foreigner what they
were being and doing.   It is this which a traveller has

to do—to observe *facts* : to draw lessons from them, if he will, but not to consider the facts in their relationship to a pre-conceived theory. Human experience is perennially important and eternally interesting; and this is what a traveller has to note and record. Political philosophies must be gathered from experience instead of (what she attempted) the real life being viewed only as related to the philosophy. In fine, her error was in treating abstractedly what was necessarily a concrete theme.

With this objection to the scheme of the book, all criticism may end. All criticism did not end (any more than it began) in this way in 1837. Speaking out so boldly as she did on a variety of the most important social topics, she naturally aroused opposition, which the power and eloquence of the style did not mitigate.

The anti-slavery tone of the book alone would have ensured violent attacks upon it and its author, as, after her ostracism because of her anti-slavery declaration, she well knew would be the case. " This subject haunts us on every page," distressfully wrote Margaret Fuller; and greatly exaggerated though this statement was, it certainly is true that there is hardly a chapter in which the reader is allowed to forget that the curse of humanity made merchandise shadowed life, directly or indirectly, throughout the whole United States. Neither by the holders of slaves in the South, nor by their accessories in the North, was it possible that she could be regarded otherwise than as an enemy, the more powerful, and therefore the more to be hated and abused, because of her standing and her ability. In estimating the courage and disinterestedness which she displayed in so decisively bearing her witness

against the state of American society under the slave
system, it must be remembered not only that she had
many valued personal friends in the South, and
amongst the Anti-Abolitionists of the North, but also
that she knew that she was closing against herself a
wide avenue for the dissemination of her opinions upon
any subject whatsoever. No book written by an
Abolitionist would be admitted into any one of
thousands of American homes. The Abolitionists reprinted portions of *Society of America*, as a pamphlet,
and distributed it broadcast. The result was that, up
to the time when slavery was abolished Harriet Martineau was continually held up to scorn and reprobation
in Southern newspapers, "in the good company of
Mrs. Chapman and Mrs. Harriet Beecher Stowe."

Even greater courage was displayed by Harriet
Martineau in her boldness of utterance upon some
other points, about which freedom of thought was
as obnoxious in England as in America. When she
maintained that divorce should be permissible by
mutual consent, provided only that the interests of
children and the distribution of property were equit-
ably arranged for; when she pleaded for the emanci-
pation of women; or when she devoted a chapter to
showing the evils which spring from the accumulation
of enormous fortunes, and incidentally attacked the
laws and customs of primogeniture, of the transfer
of land, and the like, which are devised specially to
facilitate and encourage such accumulations: in these
and other passages of an equally radical nature, she
braved a large body of opinion in English society, as
well as in the other country for which she wrote.
She mentions subsequently, that for many years she
was occasionally startled by finding herself regarded

in various quarters as a free-thinker upon dangerous subjects, and as something of a demagogue. I have little doubt that the "advanced" political philosophy of *Society in America* did originate such suspicions in minds of the Conservative order, "the timid party," as she described them in this same book. Yet she adds:

I have never regretted its boldness of speech. I felt a relief in having opened my mind which I would at no time have exchanged for any gain of reputation or fortune. The time had come when, having experienced what might be called the extremes of obscurity and difficulty first, and influence and success afterwards, I could pronounce that there was nothing for which it was worth sacrificing freedom of thought and speech.

There was but little in *Society in America* of the ordinary book of travels. As an account of the political condition and the social arrangements of the American people it was of singular value. But the personal incidents of travel, the descriptions of scenery, the reminiscences of eminent persons, of all which Harriet Martineau had gathered a store, were entirely omitted from this work. Messrs. Saunders and Otley suggested to her that she should make a second book out of this kind of material. She consented; and wrote her *Retrospect of Western Travel.* She completed the manuscript of this in December 1837, and it was published soon afterwards in three volumes. The publishers gave her six hundred pounds for it.

The fifteen hundred pounds which she thus earned exceeded in amount the whole of what she had then received for her *Illustrations of Political Economy.* The last-named great work was nearly all published upon the absurdly unequal terms which Charles Fox had secured from her in the beginning. It was characteristic of her generosity in pecuniary matters, and her loyalty to her friends, that although her agreement with Fox was dissoluble at the end of every five numbers, she nevertheless allowed it to hold good, and permitted him to pocket a very leonine share of her earnings throughout the whole publication of the original series, only claiming a revision of the terms when she commenced afresh, as it were, with the " Poor Law," and " Taxation " Tales. Thus the immense popularity of the *Illustrations* had not greatly enriched her. A portion of her earnings by them was invested in her American tour; and now that she received this return from her books of travels she felt it her duty to make a provision for the future. She purchased a deferred annuity of one hundred pounds to begin in April 1850. It displayed a characteristic calm confidence in herself that she should thus have entirely locked up her earnings for twelve years. She clearly felt a quiet assurance that her brain and her hand would serve to maintain her, at least as long as she was in the flower of her age.

The six volumes about America were not the whole of her work during the first eighteen months after her return to England. She wrote an article on Miss Sedgwick's works for the *Westminster Review*, and several other short papers for various magazines. The extraordinary industry with which she returned to labour after her long rest requires no comment.

Early in 1838 she wrote a work called *How to Observe in Morals and Manners*. It forms a crown octavo volume of two hundred and thirty-eight pages, and was published by Mr. Charles Knight. The book is an interesting one, both for the reflections which it contains upon the subject of its title, and as in-

dicating the method which she had herself pursued
in her study of the morals and manners of the
country in which she had been travelling. There is
certainly no failure in the courage with which she
expresses her convictions. She admits elsewhere that
the abuse which she received from America had so
acted upon her mind that she had come to quail at
the sight of letters addressed in a strange handwriting,
or of newspapers sent from the United States. But
there is no trace in this her next considerable work
of any tendency to follow rather than to lead the
public opinion of her time. One paragraph only may
be quoted to indicate this fact.

> Persecution for opinion is always going on. It can be inflicted
> out of the province of Law as well as through it. . . . Whatever
> a nation may tell him of its love of liberty should go for little if he
> sees a virtuous man's children taken from him on the ground of his
> holding an unusual religious belief; or citizens mobbed for assert-
> ing the rights of negroes; or moralists treated with public scorn
> for carrying out allowed principles to their ultimate issues; or
> scholars oppressed for throwing new light on the sacred text; or
> philosophers denounced for bringing fresh facts to the surface of
> human knowledge, whether they seem to agree or not with long
> established suppositions.*

The next piece of work that Harriet did in this
spring of 1838 was of a very different order. The
Poor Law Commissioners were desirous of issuing a
series of " Guides to Service," and application was
made to Miss Martineau to write some of these little
books. She undertook *The Maid of All Work, The
Housemaid, The Lady's Maid,* and *The Dress-maker.*
These were issued without her name on the title-page,
but the authorship was an open secret.

She was a thoroughly good housekeeper herself.

* *How to Observe,* p. 204.

Her conscience went into this, as into all her other
business. "Housewifery is supposed to transact
itself," she wrote; "but in reality it requires all the
faculties which can be brought to bear upon it, and
all the good, moral habits which conscience can originate." It was in this spirit that she wrote instructions for servants. The fine moral tone invariably
discoverable in her works is as delightful here as
elsewhere. But the little "Guides to Service," contain also the most precise and practical directions for
the doing of the household duties and the needle-work
which fall to the hands of the classes of servants for
whom she wrote. Practical hints are given from
which the majority of these classes of women-workers
might learn much; for *brains tell* in the mean and
dirty scrubbery of life as well as in pleasanter things,
and science is to be applied to common domestic
duties as to bigger undertakings. The heart and
mind of Harriet Martineau were equal to teaching
upon matters such as these, as well as to studying the
deeper relations of mankind in Political Economy, or
the state of society in a foreign land. Her great
power of sympathy enabled her to enter fully into
every human position. So well was the maid-of-all-
work's station described, and her duties indicated, and
her trials pointed out, and how she might solace herself under those troubles discovered, and the way in
which her work should be set about detailed, that the
rumour spread pretty widely that Harriet had once
occupied such a situation herself. She regarded this
mistake with complacency, as a tribute to the practical
character of her little work.

As a fact, she was herself a capable housewife. Her
housekeeping was always well done. Her own hands,

indeed, as well as her head, were employed in it on occasion. When in her home, she daily filled her lamp herself. She dusted her own books, too, invariably. Sometimes she did more. Soon after her establishment at the Lakes (an event which we have not yet reached, but the anecdote is in place here), a lady who greatly reverenced her for her writings called upon her in her new home, accompanied by a gentleman friend. As the visitors approached the house by the carriage-drive, they saw someone perched on a set of kitchen steps, cleaning the drawing-room windows. It was the famous authoress herself! She calmly went for her trumpet, to listen to their business; and when they had introduced themselves, she asked them in, and entered into an interesting conversation on various literary topics. Before they left, she explained, with evident amusement at having been caught at her housemaid's duties, that the workmen had been long about the house; that this morning, when the dirty windows might for the first time be cleaned, one of her servants had gone off to marry a carpenter, and the other to see the ceremony; and so the mistress, tired of the dirt, had set to work to wash and polish her window for herself.

An article on " Domestic Service," for the *Westminster Review* was written easily, while her mind was so full of the subject, in the beginning of June 1838. But a great enterprise was before her—a novel; and at length she settled down to this, beginning it on her thirty-sixth birthday, June 12th, 1838. The writing of this new book was interrupted by a tour in Scotland during August and September, and by writing a remarkable and eloquent article on slavery, "The Martyr Age of the United States," which occupies fifty-five pages of the *Westminster Review* in the January, 1839, number of that publication. The novel got finished, however, in February of this latter year; and it was published by Easter under the title of *Deerbrook*.

Great expectations had been entertained by the literary public of Harriet Martineau's first novel. The excellences of her *Illustrations* as works of fiction had been so marked and so many, that it was anticipated that she might write a novel of the highest order when released from the trammels under which she wrote those tales. To most of those who had expected so much *Deerbrook* was a complete disappointment. I believe I may justly say that it is the weakest of all Harriet Martineau's writings. It is, indeed, far superior in all respects to nine hundred out of every thousand novels published. But she is not judged by averages. A far higher standard of literary art is that to which we expect Harriet Martineau's writings to conform.

The book is deficient in story. Deerbrook is a country village, where two sisters from Birmingham, Hester and Margaret Ibbotson, take up their temporary abode. Mr. Hope, the village surgeon, falls in love with Margaret; but being told that Hester loves him, while Margaret is attached to Philip Enderby, Hope decides to propose to Hester; is accepted, married to the sister he does not love, and sets up housekeeping with the sister with whom he *is* in love as an inmate of his home. The wife, moreover, is of a jealous, exacting disposition, ever on the watch for some token of neglect of her feelings by her friends, anxious, irritable, and hyper-sensitive.

Here is a situation which, the characters being what they are described to be, could in real life eventuate only in either violent tragedy or long, slow heartbreak. A woman of ultra-sensitive and refined feelings could not live with a husband and a sister under such circumstances without discovering the truth. A man of active temperament and warm emotions, who declares to himself on the night of his return from his wedding tour that his marriage "has been a mistake, that he has desecrated his own home, and doomed to withering the best affections of his nature,"—such a man, with the woman he really loves living in his home, beside the unloved wife, could not completely conceal his state of mind from everybody, and presently find that after all he likes the one he has married best. Yet in the impossible manner just indicated do all things end in *Deerbrook*. The interest of the book is then suddenly shifted to Margaret and Enderby. Hope and Hester become mere accessories. But the plot does not improve. The Deerbrook people, hitherto adorers of their doctor, suddenly take to throwing stones at him, and to mobbing his house, because he votes for the Parliamentary candidate opposed by the great man of the village, and because they take it into their heads (not a particle of reason why they do so being shown) that he anatomises bodies from the graveyard. We are invited to believe that though his practice had been singularly successful, all his patients deserted him; and notwithstanding that Hester and Margaret had each seventy pounds a year of private income, the household was thus reduced to such distress that they could not afford gloves, and had to part with all their servants, and dined as a rule off potatoes and bread and butter! Then Margaret's lover, Enderby, hears that she and Hope loved each other before Hope married; and though he does not for a moment suspect anything wrong in the present, and though he pas-

sionately loves Margaret, this supposed discovery that
he is not her first love causes him to peremptorily
and without explanation break off the engagement.
Presently, however, an epidemic comes and restores
confidence in Mr. Hope; and Enderby's sister, who had
given him the information on which he acted, con-
fesses that she had exaggerated the facts and invented
part of her story; and so it all ends, and they live
happily ever after !

Feeble and untrue as are plot and characters in this
"poor novel" (as Carlyle without injustice called it),
yet many scenes are well written, the details are truly
coloured, and every page is illuminated with thought
of so high an order and language so brilliant, so
flowing, so felicitous, that one forgives, for the sake of
merits such as these, the failure of the fiction to be
either true or interesting. This seemed to show,
nevertheless, that Harriet could write essays, and
travels, and didactic and philosophical works, but
could not write a novel except "with a purpose,"
when the accomplishment of the purpose might excuse
any other shortcomings. But when one considers the
great excellence of many of the *Illustrations,* the decided
drawing of the characters, the truthful analysis of the
springs of human action, the manner in which the
incidents are combined and arranged to develop and
display dispositions and histories, it becomes clear that
she *had* great powers as an imaginative depicter of
human nature and social life, and that there must have
been other causes than sheer incapacity for the faults
and the feeblenesses of *Deerbrook.*

The first cause was what seems to me a mistaken
theory about plots in fiction, which she had adopted
since writing the *Illustrations.* She now fancied

that a perfect plot *must* be taken from life, forgetting
that we none of us know the whole plot of the existence of any other creature than ourselves, and that
the psychological insight of the gifted novelist is displayed in arguing from what is known to what is
unknown, and in combining the primary elements
of human character into their necessary consequences
in act and feeling. This error she would have been
cured from by experience had she gone on writing
fiction. She might have been aided in this by what
she naïvely enough avows about *Deerbrook* : that she
supposed that she took the story of Hope's marriage
from the history of a friend of her family, and that
she afterwards found out that nothing of the sort had
really happened to him ! She might then have asked
herself whether the story as she had told it was more
possible than it was possible that gunpowder should
be put to flame without an explosion ? A girl in her
teens might have been forgiven for playing with the
history of the wildest passions of the human heart ;
but Harriet Martineau erred because she tried to
enslave herself to fact in a matter in which she should
have inferred, judged from psychological principles,
and trusted to the intuitions of her own mind for the
final working out of her problem. As it was, if her
" fact " had been a reality, we should have been compelled to account for the placid progress of events by
the supposition that she had utterly misrepresented
the characters of the persons involved.

This bondage to (supposed) fact was one cause of
her failure. A lesser, but still important reason for it,
was that she tried to imitate Jane Austen's style.
Her admiration of the works of this mistress of the
art of depicting human nature was very great. Har-

riet's diary of the period when she was preparing to write *Deerbrook,* shows that she re-read Miss Austen's novels, and found them " wonderfully beautiful." This judgment she annexed to *Emma*; and again, after recording her new reading of *Pride and Prejudice,* she added, " I think it as clever as before; but Miss Austen seems wonderfully afraid of pathos. I long to try." When she did " try," she, either intentionally or unconsciously, but very decidedly, modelled her style on Miss Austen's. But the two women were essentially different. Harriet Martineau had an original mind ; she did wrong, and prepared the retribution of failure for herself, in imitating at all; and Jane Austen was one of the last persons she should have imitated.

The principal reasons for the inferiority of *Deerbrook,* however, are found in her personal history. Three months after its publication, she was utterly prostrated by an illness which had undoubtedly been slowly growing upon her for long before. Thus, she wrote her novel under the depression and failure of strength caused by this malady. The illness itself was partly the result of what further tended to make her work poor in quality—the domestic anxieties, miseries, and heart-burnings of that period.

The three anxious members of her family were at this time upon her hands. That brother who had succeeded to the father's business, and in whose charge it had failed, was at this time in London. Before the weaving business stopped, Henry Martineau was engaged ; but the girl broke off the affair in consequence of the downfall of his pecuniary prospects. Henry then undertook a wine-merchant's business, and, wretched with the mortification of his double failure in purse and in heart, he yielded to the temptations of his new employment, and became intemperate. During the time that *Deerbrook* was being written, he was living with his mother and sister in London. At the same time Mrs. Martineau, now nearing seventy years old, was becoming blind. The natural irritability of her temper was thus increased. The heart-wearing trials of a home with two súch inmates were made greater to Harriet by the fact that an aged aunt also lived with them, who, besides the many cares exacted for the well-being of age, added to Harriet's troubles by the necessity of shielding her from the tempers and depressions of the other two.

It was in this home that Harriet Martineau did all the work that has now been recorded after her return from America. No one who has the least conception of how imperatively necessary domestic peace and comfort are for the relief of the brain taxed with literary labour, will be surprised to hear that Harriet's strength and spirits failed during all that summer and winter in which she was writing *Deerbrook*, and that presently her health completely broke down.

# CHAPTER VII.

## FIVE YEARS OF ILLNESS AND THE MESMERIC
## RECOVERY.

ALMOST immediately after the publication of *Deer-brook* Harriet started for a Continental tour. She was
to escort an invalid cousin to Switzerland, and after-
wards to travel through Italy with two other friends.
But her illness became so severe by the time that she
reached Venice that the remainder of the journey had
to be abandoned. Under medical advice, a couch was
fitted up in the travelling carriage, and upon it, lifted
in and out at every stage, she returned to England
and was conveyed to her sister's at Newcastle-on-
Tyne. In the autumn of that same year (1839) she
took up her abode in Front Street, Tynemouth, in order
to remain under the medical care of her brother-in-law,
Mr. Greenhow, of Newcastle.

Her physical sufferings during the next five years
were very severe, and almost incessant. She could not
go out of the house, and alternated only between her
bed in one room and her couch in another. From
her sick-room window she overlooked a narrow space
of down, the ruins of the priory, the harbour with its

traffic, and the sea. On the farther side of the harbour she could discern through the telescope a railroad, a spreading heath, and, on the hills which bounded the view, two or three farms. To this outlook she, whose life had been hitherto spent so actively, and in the midst of such a throng of society, found herself confined for a term of five years. At the same time her pain was so great that she was compelled to take opiates daily. "I have observed, with inexpressible shame, that with the newspaper in my hand, no details of the peril of empires, or of the starving miseries of thousands, could keep my eye from the watch before me, or detain my attention one second beyond the time when I might have my opiate. For two years, too, I wished and intended to dispense with my opiate for once, to try how much there was to bear, and how I should bear it; but I never did it, strong as was the shame of always yielding. I am convinced that there is no more possibility of becoming inured to acute agony of body, than to paroxysms of remorse—the severest of moral pains. A familiar pain becomes more and more dreaded, instead of becoming more lightly esteemed in proportion to its familiarity. The pain itself becomes more odious, more oppressive, more feared in proportion to the accumulation of experience of weary hours, in proportion to the aggregate of painful associations which every visitation revives."[*]

Some indication of what she endured in those weary years is given in this quotation. If we had to rely upon the inferences to be drawn from the amount of work which she did in her sick-room, we should naturally suppose the suffering not to have been very great;

---

[*] *Life in the Sick Room.*

for she produced, in the midst of her illness, as much and as noble work as we look for from the most active persons in ordinary health.

The first business of the sick-room life was to write both an article for publication, and a number of letters of personal appeal to friends, on behalf of Oberlin College, an institution which was being founded in America for the education of persons of colour of both sexes, and of the students who had been turned out of Lane College for their advocacy of anti-slavery principles.

The next undertaking was another novel; or, rather, a history, imaginatively treated, of the negro revolution in San Domingo. Toussaint L'Ouverture, the leader of the revolution and the president of the black Republic of Hayti, was the hero of this story. *The Hour and the Man,* as a mere novel, is vastly superior to *Deerbrook.* Harriet wrote it, however, rather as a contribution to the same anti-slavery cause for which she had written her preceding article, believing that it would be useful to that cause to show forth the capacity and the high moral character which had been displayed by a negro of the blackest shade when in possession of power. The work was begun in May 1840, and published in November of the same year.

Lord Jeffrey, in a familiar private letter to Empson, his successor in the editorship of the *Edinburgh Review,* wrote thus of *The Hour and the Man* :—

I have read Harriet's first volume, and give in my adhesion to her Black Prince with all my heart and soul. The book is really not only beautiful and touching, but *noble* ; and I do not recollect when I have been more charmed, whether by very sweet and eloquent writing and glowing description, or by elevated as well as tender sentiments. . . . The book is calculated to make its readers better, and does great honour to the heart as well as the talent and fancy of the author.  I would go a long way to kiss the hem of her garment, or the hand that delineated this glowing and lofty representation of purity and noble virtue.  And she must not only be rescued from all debasing anxieties about her subsistence, but placed in a station of affluence and honour; though I believe she truly cares for none of these things.  It is sad to think that she suffers so much, and may even be verging to dissolution.

Even the morose and ungracious Carlyle, writing to Emerson of this book, is obliged to say "It is beautiful as a child's heart; and in so shrewd a brain!" While Florence Nightingale declares that she "can scarcely refrain from thinking of it as the greatest of historical romances."

The allusion in the latter part of Lord Jeffrey's letter was to a proposal just then made to give Harriet Martineau one of the Civil List literary pensions. This idea had been mooted first during the progress of her *Illustrations,* and again after her return from America; but upon each occasion she had stated privately that she would not be willing to accept it. She replied from Tynemouth to the same effect to Mr. Hutton, who wrote to enquire if she would now be thus assisted.  Her objection was, in the first place, one of principle; she disapproved of the money of the people being dispensed in any pensions at the sole will of the Ministry, instead of being conferred directly by the representatives of the people. Her second reason was, that after accepting she would feel herself bound to the Ministers, and would be understood by the public to be so bound, and would thus suffer a loss of both freedom and usefulness during whatever life might remain to her.  Lord Melbourne, a few months later, in July 1841, made her an explicit offer of a pension of £150 per annum, and her answer to the Minister was substantially the same as to her friend. She said that while taxation was levied so unequally, and while Parliament had no voice in the distribution of pensions, she would rather receive public aid from the parish, if necessary, than as a pensioner. She added an earnest plea that all influential persons who held themselves indebted on public grounds to any writer, would show that gratitude by endeavouring to make better copyright arrangements and foreign treaties, so as to secure to authors the full, due, and independent reward of their efforts.

The rare (perhaps mistaken) generosity of this refusal can only be appreciated by bearing in mind that she had invested a large part of her earnings a few years before in a form from which she was now receiving no return. During her illness she was really in want of money, so far as to have to accept assistance from relatives. For her charities she partly provided by doing fancy-work, sending subscriptions both in this form and in the shape of articles for publication to the anti-slavery cause in America.

In the early part of 1841 she began a series of four children's stories, which were published under the general title of *The Playfellow*. These admirable tales are still amongst the best-known and most popular of her writings; simple, vivid, and interesting, they are really model children's stories, and it would have been quite impossible for any reader to imagine that they were written by an invalid, in constant suffering. *Settlers at Home* was the first one written, *The Prince and the Peasant* came next; then *Feats on the Fjord*; and, finally, that one from which I quoted largely in an early chapter, *The Crofton Boys*. By the time the last-named was finished she was very ill, and believed that she should never write another book.

Her interest in all public affairs continued, never-theless, to be as keen as ever. In 1841 she wrote for publication a long letter to support the American Anti-Slavery Society under a secession from its ranks of a number of persons, chiefly clerical, who objected, of all things, to women being allowed to be mem-bers of the Society ! Another piece of work which she did for the public benefit was by a course of corre-spondence, full of delicate tact, to personally reconcile Sir Robert Peel and Mr. Cobden, and so to pave the way for the amicable work of the two statesmen in the Repeal of the Corn Laws.

In 1843, some of her friends who knew her circum-stances, and that she had refused a pension, collected money to present her with a testimonial. £1,400, thus obtained, was invested for her benefit in the Terminable Long Annuities, and a considerable sum besides was expended in a present of plate. The Ladies Lambton (the eldest of whom, as Countess of Elgin, was afterwards one of her warmest friends) went over to Tynemouth to use the plate with her for the first time, and " it was a testimonial fête."

It was about this time, too, that the personal acquaintance, destined to become an intimate associa-tion in work, between Harriet Martineau and Flo-rence Nightingale was commenced. Miss Martineau's younger sister Ellen had been governess in Miss Nightingale's family. Sick-nursing occupied Florence Nightingale's hands and heart long before the Crimean War made her famous, and Harriet Martineau was one of the sick to whom she ministered in those earlier days.

Towards the end of 1843, Harriet's mind had accu-mulated a store of thoughts and feelings which imperatively pressed to be poured forth. She wrote then, in about six weeks, her volume of essays, *Life in the Sick-Room.* The book was published under the pseudonym of " An Invalid," but was immediately attributed to her on all hands. It is a most interesting record of the high thoughts and feelings by which so melancholy an experience as years of suffering, of an apparently hopeless character, can be elevated, and made productive of benefit to the sufferer's own nature. Incidentally there is much wise counsel in the volume for those who have the care of invalids of this class.

Amidst the many expressions of admiration and interest which this work drew forth, the following is perhaps most worthy of preservation because of the source whence it came. Mr. Quillinan, Wordsworth's son-in-law, wrote as follows to his friend, Henry Crabbe Robinson, on December 9th, 1843 :—

Mr. Wordsworth, Mrs. Wordsworth, and Miss Fenwick have been quite charmed, affected, and instructed by the invalid's volume. . . . Mrs. Wordsworth, after a few pages were read, at once pronounced it to be Miss Martineau's production, and concluded that you knew all about it and caused it to be sent hither. In some of its most eloquent parts it stops short of their wishes and expectations : but they all agree that it is *a rare book,* doing honour to the head and heart of your able and interesting friend. Mr. Wordsworth praised it with more unreserve—I may say, with more *earnestness*—than is usual with him. The serene and heavenly-minded Miss Fenwick was prodigal of her admiration. But Mrs. Wordsworth's was the crowning praise. She said—and you know how she would say it—" I wish I had read exactly such a book as that years ago ! " . . . It is a *genuine* and touching series of meditations by an invalid not sick in mind or heart.*

From one of the letters with which Mr. Henry G. Atkinson has favoured me and my readers, I find that she wrote a chapter for that book, which un-

* *Diary and Letters of H. C. Robinson,* vol. iii. p. 235.

doubtedly must have been of the deepest interest,
but which was not published.

LETTER TO MR. ATKINSON.

[Extract.]                                November 19, 1872.

DEAR FRIEND,

. . . You will feel at once how earnestly I must be longing
for death—I who never loved life, and who would any day of my
life have rather departed than stayed. Well ! it can hardly go on
very much longer now. But I do wish it was permitted to us to
judge for ourselves a little how long we ought to carry on the task
which we never desired and could not refuse, and how soon we
may fairly relieve our comrades from the burden of taking care of
us. I wonder whether the chapter I wrote about this for the
" Sick Room " book will ever see the light. I rather wish it may,
because I believe it utters what many people think and feel. I let
it be omitted from that book because it might perhaps injure the
impression of the rest of the volume ; but, so far as I remember
it, it is worth considering, and therefore publishing.

I have made such enquiries as I could (of one of
Miss Martineau's executors and others), but can get
no tidings of this missing chapter on Euthanasia. It
was just such a subject—needing for its discussion,
courage, calmness, common-sense, and logic, combined
with sympathy, and a high standard of moral beauty
and goodness—as she would have been sure to treat
rarely well. There is one passage in *Life in the Sick-
Room*, bearing upon the question ; she observes that
the great reason why hopeless invalids so commonly
endure on when they are longing for the rest of insensibility, is the uncertainty as to whether they may not
find themselves still conscious in another state. Her
own history was to supply a stronger reason still
against irrevocable action being taken upon our rash
assumptions that our work and our usefulness in life are
ended. As she truly observed : " No one knows when
the spirits of men begin to work, or when they leave

off, or whether they work best when their bodies are weak, or when they are strong. Every human creature that has a spirit in him must therefore be taken care of, and kept alive as long as possible, that his spirit may do all it can in the world." So she wrote at that very time—showing how her mind was pondering every view of the subject.

The sentence just quoted is from *Dawn Island,* a little one-hundred paged story which she wrote in the midst of her suffering, as her contribution to the funds of the Anti-Corn Law League. It was printed, and sold, for the benefit of that League, at the great bazaar of 1845.

After the publication of the "Sick-Room" book, she commenced the writing of her autobiography—not as it was published afterwards, be it understood—for she was too ill to make much progress with it, and soon stopped writing. But she *never* became too ill to feel and to show a vivid interest in every cause that had the happiness and progress of mankind for its object. She kept up an extensive correspondence with those engaged in the world's work, and such personal efforts for public objects as those above mentioned she frequently exerted—sometimes over-exerted—herself to make. Her body was chained to two small rooms; but her mind, with all its powers and affections, yet swept freely through the universe. No one would have been more impatient than she herself of any pretence that she lived incessantly on a high plane of lofty emotions, where pain ceased to be felt, or that her care for others was so extraordinary that self-regard was swallowed up in the depths of altruism. I have quoted her candid revelations about her sufferings and her opiates, to avoid the possibility of conveying

an impression that she was thus guilty of hypocrisy
or affectation. But the wide interests and the sympathies with mankind that were the solace of her sick
life, and the inspiration of the work which she did so
heavily, and yet so continuously, amidst her pain,
assuredly shall be marked with the reverence that they
merit.

In 1844 the long illness came to an end. Harriet
Martineau was restored to perfect health by means of
mesmerism. Such a cure of such a person could not
fail to make a great sensation. Not only had she a
wide circle of personal acquaintances, but she had
deeply impressed the public at large with a sense of
her perfect sanity, her calm common-sense, and her
practical wisdom, as well as with a conviction of her
truthfulness and accuracy. Accordingly, as the *Zoist*
(Dr. Elliotson's mesmeric periodical) declared at the
time :—

The subject which the critic, a few months since, would not con-
descend to notice, has been elevated to a commanding position.
It is the topic with which the daily papers and the weekly periodicals are filled ; in fact, all classes are moved by one common consent, and mesmerism, from the palace to the smallest town in the
United Kingdom, is the scientific question absorbing public attention. . . . The immediate cause of all this activity is the publication
of the case of Miss Martineau, who, after five years' incessant
suffering and confinement to her couch, is now well.

I have thought that what needs to be said here of
the medical aspect and course of this period of suffering, and of the final cure, will best be said consecu-
tively ; and, therefore, we will look back briefly over the
five busy but suffering years, the work of which has
now been recorded, and see what were the physical
conditions under which that work was executed.

Her health had been declining gradually from 1834

to 1839; there was a slow but a marked deterioration in strength, and her spirits became depressed. In April of the latter year, when she undertook a continental journey, the fatigue of travelling suddenly aggravated her condition; and in Venice, early in June, she was compelled to consult a physician, Dr. Nardo. She was found to be suffering from a tumour, with enlargement and displacement of an important organ, all this causing great internal pain, accompanied by frequent weakening hæmorrhages. She was carried back to England by easy stages, and lying on a couch, and reached Newcastle-on-Tyne at the end of July 1839. She stayed for some time at the house in that town of her eldest sister, and then was removed only nine miles off, in order that her brother-in-law, Mr. T. M. Greenhow, F.R.C.S., might undertake the medical care of her case. Until October, she persevered in taking walking exercise; but the pain, sickness, and breathlessness which accompanied this were so distressing, that soon after her removal to Tynemouth she ceased to go out of doors, or even to descend the stairs.

Mr. Greenhow's prescriptions were confined at first to opiates, and other medicines to alleviate symptoms. The opiates were not taken in excess—as, indeed, the books written in the period would conclusively prove. The patient's suffering was so great, however, that extreme recourse to such palliatives might have been forgiven. She could not raise the right leg; and could neither sit up for the faintness which then ensued, nor lie down with ease because of the pains in her back. "She could not sleep at night till she devised a plan of sleeping under a basket, for the purpose of keeping the weight of the bed-clothes from her; and even then she was scared by horrors all night, and reduced by sickness during the day. This sickness increased to such a degree that for two years she was extremely low from want of food."

At the end of two years, that is to say, in Septembei 1841, Sir Charles Clarke, M.D., was called in consultation ; and he prescribed iodine, remarking at the same time that, in his view, such a case as hers was practically incurable, and admitting that he " had tried iodine in an infinite number of such cases, and never knew it avail." For the next *three years* Miss Martineau took three grains per diem of iodide of iron. It relieved the sickness; but up to April 1844 (two and a half years from the commencement of its administration), Mr. Greenhow did not pretend that any improvement in the physical condition had taken place. In that month, as he afterwards said, he believed he found a slight change, " but he was not sure "; and, if any, it was very trifling. The patient, on her part, was quite convinced that her state then was in no way altered.

More than once different friends—amongst them Lord Lytton, Mr. Hallam, and the Basil Montagus— had urged her to try mesmerism; but she had thought it due to her relative to give his orthodox medicines the fullest trial, before taking herself out of hio hauds in such a way. In June 1844, however, Mr. Greenhow himself suggested that she should be mesmerised. Of course, so advised, she consented to make the trial. A Mr. Hall, brought by Mr. Greenhow, accordingly mesmerised her for the first time on June 22nd, 1844, and again on the following day.

The patient thought she experienced some relief, but did not feel quite sure. " On occasion of a per-

fectly new experience, scepticism and self-distrust are
strong."* The next day, however, set her doubts at
rest. Mr. Hall was unable to come to her, and she
asked her maid to make the passes in his stead.

> Within one minute, the twilight and phosphoric lights appeared;
> and in two or three more a delicious sensation of ease spread
> through me—a cool comfort, before which all pain and distress
> gave way, oozing out, as it were, at the soles of my feet. During
> that hour, and almost the whole evening, I could no more help
> exclaiming with pleasure than a person in torture crying out with
> pain. I became hungry, and ate with relish for the first time for
> five years. There was no heat, oppression, or sickness during the
> *séance*, nor any disorder afterwards. During the whole evening,
> instead of the lazy, hot ease of opiates, under which pain is felt to
> lie in wait, I experienced something of the indescribable sensations
> of health, which I had quite lost and forgotten.

Her dear friend during all the years that remained
to her—Mr. Henry G. Atkinson†—had just come into
her life. His interest in her case was enlisted by
their mutual friend, Basil Montagu; and Mr. Atkinson
undertook to direct the mesmeric treatment by correspondence. Margaret, the maid, continued the mes-

* This and the succeeding quotations are from her "Letters on
Mesmerism," published in the *Athenæum*, 1845.

† As this friendship had a profound influence upon Harriet's
after thought and work, some description of Mr. Atkinson seems in
place; and I need offer that gentleman no apology for merely
quoting what has appeared in print before about him. Margaret
Fuller wrote thus of him in a private letter, in 1846:—

"Mr. Atkinson is a man about thirty, in the fulness of his
powers, tall and finely formed, with a head for Leonardo to paint;
mild and composed, but powerful and sagacious; he does not think,
but perceives and acts. He is intimate with artists, having studied
architecture himself as a profession; but has some fortune on which
he lives. Sometimes stationary and acting in the affairs of other
men; sometimes wandering about the world and learning; he
seems bound by no tie, yet looks as if he had relatives in every
place."—*Memoirs of Margaret Fuller*, by Emerson.

merism till September, and then Mr. Atkinson induced
his friend Mrs. Montague Wynyard, the young widow
of a clergyman, to undertake the case. "In pure
zeal and benevolence this lady came to me, and has
been with me ever since. When I found myself able
to repose on the knowledge and power (mental and
moral) of my mesmerist the last impediments to my progress were cleared away and I improved accordingly."

On December the 6th Mr. Greenhow found his patient
quite well, and about to leave the place of her im-
prisonment, and start on a series of friendly visits.
He declared, notwithstanding, that, firstly, her *physical
condition* was not essentially different from what it
had been all through; secondly, that the change in
her *sensations* arose from the iodine suddenly and
miraculously becoming more effective, and not from
mesmerism.

Such is the medical history, so interesting to all
physiological students and to all sufferers of the same
class, of Harriet Martineau's five years' illness and
recovery. My business is simply to state facts, and
I need not here undertake any dissertation upon mesmerism. It is sufficient to add that only those who
are unaware of the profundity of our ignorance (up
to the present day) about the action of the nervous
system, and still more about what *life* really is, can be
excused for rash jeering and hasty incredulity in such
a case as this.

Harriet Martineau knew that she was well again,
and it seemed to her a clear duty to make as public
as possible the history of how her recovery had been
brought about. She did so by six letters to the
*Athenæum*; and these were reprinted in pamphlet form.
Mr. Greenhow was thereupon guilty of one of the most

serious professional faults possible. He also published
an account of *The Case of Miss H. M.,* in a shil-
ling pamphlet, giving the most minute and painful
details of her illness, and respecting no confidence
that had been reposed in his medical integrity. The
result of this conduct on his part was that his patient
felt herself compelled to break off all future intercourse
with a man capable of such objectionable action.

It may be added here that the cure was a permanent one.* She enjoyed ten years of health so good
that she declared it taught her that in no previous
period of her life had she ever been well. It may be
as well to say that she never wavered in her assurance
that her cure was worked by mesmerism, and that the
cure was complete. All dispute about her firm conviction on this point may be set at rest by the following
extracts from—

LETTERS TO MR. ATKINSON.

[Extract.] July 6th, 1874.

Notices of my mesmeric experience in illness have revived an
anxiety of mine about what may happen when I am gone, if certain
parties should bring up the old falsehoods again, when 'I am not
here to assert and prove the truth. I don't in the least suppose
you can help me, any more than Mrs. Chapman, whom I have got

---

* I find there is a widespread impression that she eventually
died of the same tumour that she supposed to have been cured
at this time. It should be distinctly stated, however, that if
this were the case, Mr. Greenhow and Sir C. Clarke were both
*utterly* wrong in their diagnosis in 1840. I have read Mr. Greenhow's *Report of the Case of Miss H. M.,* and the notes of the
post-mortem lie before me—kindly lent me by the surgeon, Mr.
King, now of Bedford Park, who made the autopsy. I find that
the organ which Mr. Greenhow and his consultant both stated
to be the seat of the disease, enlargement, and tumour, in 1840, is
described as being found " particularly small and unaffected " after
death.

to look over a box of papers of mine deposited with her. But I had rather tell you what is on my mind about it.

I wrote, at Tynemouth, a diary of my case and experience under the mesmeric experiment (experiment desired and proposed by Mr. Greenhow himself). *He* read it when finished, and so did several of my friends. There are two copies somewhere, for, not wishing to show certain passages, rather saucy, about the Green-how prejudices and behaviour, I accepted Mrs. Wynyard's kind offer to copy the MS., omitting those remarks. Now where are those MSS. ? I cannot find them, nor say what I did with them, beyond having a dim notion that they (or at least Mrs. Wynyard's copy) were put away into some safe place, to await future chances. I perfectly remember the look of the packet, and the label on it, &c. When I remember what was said after reading it, by one of the wisest people I have known, I am *shocked* at our inability to find it. " One must dispute anything being the cause of anything, if one disputes, after reading this statement, that your recovery is due to mesmerism." And now, while I see false statements of the " facts," and false references circulating, as at present, I can-not find my own narrative, written from day to day, and do not know where to turn next! If I had strength I would turn out all the papers in my possession, and make sure for myself. Now, dear friend, do you think you ever saw that statement ?

[Extract.]                                September 18, 1874.

My malady was absolutely unlike cancer, and it never had any sort of relation to " malignant " disease. The doctors called it "indolent tumour—most probably polypus." Don't you remember how, at that very time, the great dispute on Elliotson's hands was whether any instance could be adduced of cure of organic disease by mesmerism ? Elliotson was nearly certain, but not quite, of the cure of a cancer case in his own practice. The doctors were full of the controversy, and some of them wrote both to me and to Mr. Greenhow to enquire the nature of my case, whether malignant or not. Of course we both replied " No." It would be a dreadful misfortune if now anybody concerned should tell a different story. Greenhow is still living (aged 82) and all alive; and he would like nothing better than to get hold of it, and bring out another indecent pamphlet. If I could but lay hands on the diary of the case, written at the time, what a security it would be ? `But I can nowhere find it. The next best security is turning back to the statement, " Letters" in the *Athenæum* of the autumn of 1844. Those " Letters " went through two editions when reprinted, after having carried those numbers of the *Athenæum* through three editions. One would think the narrative must be accessible enough. Above all things, let there be no mistake in our statements.

It ought to be enough for observers that I had ten years of robust health after that recovery, walking from sixteen to twenty miles in a day, on occasion, and riding a camel in the heart of Nubia and hundreds of miles on horseback, through Palestine to Damascus, and back to the Levant.

I have written so much because I could not help it. I shall hardly do it again. I will add only that the mesmerising began in June 1844, and the cure was effected before the following Christmas.

Dear friend,

I am yours ever,

H. M.

# CHAPTER VIII.

## THE HOME LIFE.

At forty-two years old, Harriet Martineau found herself
free for the first time to form and take possession of a
*home of her own.* Now, for the first time, she could
have the luxury which many girls obtain by marriage
so young that they spoil it to themselves and others,
and which it is as natural for each grown woman to
desire, irrespective of marriage, as it is for a fledged
bird to leave the old nest—a house and a domestic
circle in which she could be the organising spirit,
where the home arrangements should be of her own
ordering, and where she could have the privacy and
the self-management which can no otherwise be enjoyed, in combination with the exercise of that house-
wifely skill to which all women more or less incline.

The beauty of the scenery led her to fix upon the
English Lakes for the locality in which to make her
home, and, finding no suitable house vacant, she resolved to build one for herself. She purchased two
acres of land, within half-a-mile of the village of
Ambleside; borrowed some money on mortgage from
a well-to-do cousin; had the plans drawn out under

her own instructions, and watched the house being built so that it should suit her own tastes.

It is a pretty little gabled house, built of grey stone, and stands upon a small rocky eminence—whence its name, " The Knoll." There is enough rock to hold the house, and to allow the formation of a terrace about twenty feet wide in front of the windows; then there comes the descent of the face of the rock. At the foot of the rock is the garden. Narrow flights of steps at either end of the terrace lead down to the greensward and the flower-beds; in the centre of these is a grey granite sun-dial, with the characteristic motto around it—" Come Light! Visit me!" To the left is the gardener's cottage, with the cow-house, pig-stye, and root-shed. The front of the house looks across the garden, and over the valley to Loughrigg. Its back is turned to the road, and concealed from passers-by, partly by the growth of greenery, and partly by the Methodist Chapel. A winding path leads up from the road to the house, and a small path forking off from this goes round past the cottage to the field where the cows used to graze, and to the piece of land that was appropriated to growing the roots for the cows and the household fruit and vegetables.

Within, " The Knoll" is just a nice little residence for a maiden lady, with her small household, and room for an occasional guest. You enter by a covered porch and find the drawing room on the right hand of the hall. It is a fairly large room, and remarkably well-lighted; there was a window-tax when she built, but she showed her faith in the growth of political common-sense abrogating so mischievous an impost, by building in anticipation of freedom of light and air from taxation. The drawing-room has two large windows, one of which descends quite to the floor, and is provided with two or three stone steps outside, so that the inmates may readily step forth on to the terrace. This window, by the way, exposed her to another tax than the Government one. Hunters of celebrities were wont, in the tourist season, not merely to walk round her garden and terrace without leave, but even to mount these steps and flatten the tips of their noses against her window. Objectionable as the liability to this friendly attention would be felt by most of us, it was doubly so to Miss Martineau because of her deafness, which precluded her from receiving warning of her admirers' approaches from the crunching of their footsteps on the gravel—so that the first intimation that she would receive of their presence would be to turn her head by chance and find the flattened nose and the peering eyes against the window-pane. There is a special record of one occasion, when her bell rang in an agitated fashion, and the maid, on going, found her mistress much disturbed. " There is a *big* woman, with a *big* pattern on her dress, beckoning to me to come to the window—go, and tell her to go away." But similar incidents were manifold, and her servants had to be trained to guard their mistress as if she were the golden apples of the Hesperides. Indeed, for several years (till she became too ill to travel) she used to leave her lake-side home altogether during the tourist season.

In her latest years she commonly wrote in the drawing-room, as the sunniest and most cheerful apartment, and where, too, she could sit by the fire, and yet get plenty of daylight. Her proper study, however, was the room on the opposite side of the

hall. This is a long room with a bay window at the
other end from the fire-place, and the door in the
centre. Book-cases lined the whole of these walls;
but her library was an extensive one, and there were
books all over the house. This room served as
dining-room and study, both; the writing-table was
near the window, the dining-table farther towards
the fire.

The only other room on the ground floor is the
kitchen, which runs parallel with the drawing-room.
Her principles and her practice went hand-in-hand
in her domestic arrangements as in her life generally;
and her kitchen was as airy, light, and comfortable
for her maids as her drawing-room for herself. The
kitchen, too, was provided with a book-case for a
servants' library. A scullery, dairy, &c. are annexed
to the kitchen, and the entrance to the cellars below is
also found through the green-baize door which shuts
off the cooking region from the front of the house.

Up-stairs, that which was her own room is large
and cheerful, and provided with two windows, a big
hanging-cupboard, and a good-sized dressing-room—
the latter, indeed, fully large enough for a maid
to sleep in. The next was the spare-room; and there
lingers no small interest about the guest-chamber,
where Harriet Martineau received such guests as
Charlotte Brontë, George Eliot, Emerson, and Douglas
Jerrold. A small servant's room is next to this, and
a larger one is over the kitchen, so that it comes
just at the head of the stairs. Such is the size and
arrangement of Harriet Martineau's home.

Climbing plants soon covered "The Knoll" on every
side. The ivy kept it green through all the year; the
porch was embowered in honeysuckle, clematis, passion-

flower, and Virginia creeper. Wordsworth, Macready, and other friends of note, planted trees for Harriet below the terrace. The making of all these arrangements was a source of satisfaction and delight to her such as can only be imagined by those who have felt what it is to come abroad after a long and painful confinement from illness, and to find life and usefulness freely open again under agreeable conditions and prospects.

While her house was being built, she lodged in Ambleside; and in that time, during the autumn and winter of 1845-6, she wrote her *Forest and Game Law Tales*, with the object of showing how mischievous the Game Laws were in their operation upon society at large, and more particularly upon the fortunes of individual farmers, and upon the labourers who were led into poaching. These tales occupy three volumes of the ordinary novel size. They had a sale which would have been very good for a novel; two thousand copies were disposed of, and, doubtless, did some service for the cause for which she had worked. So far as her own pecuniary interests were concerned, however, these tales made her first failure. It was the only work which never returned her any remuneration. The publisher had reckoned on a very large circulation, and so had put out too much capital in stock, stereotypes, and the like, to leave any profit on the sale that actually took place; and the publication unfortunately coincided with the agitation of the political world about the repeal of the Corn Laws. But one pleasing incident arose out of them for her personally. She had been in difficulties as to how to obtain turf to lay down upon the land under her terrace. One fine morning, soon after her entrance on her home, her

maid found a great heap of sods under the window,
when she opened the shutters in the morning. A
dirty note, closed with a wafer, was stuck upon the
pile; and this was found to state that the sods were
" a token of gratitude for the Game Law Tales, from a
Poacher." Harriet never discovered from whom this
tribute came.

She took possession of her home on April 7th, 1846.
During the summer, she wrote another story for
young people—one of her most interesting tales, and
instructive in its moral bearing—*The Billow and the
Rock.* It must here be noted, in passing, that this is
the last of her works in which the Theism that she
had, up to this time, held for religious truth, makes
itself visible. A new experience was about to lead
her to think afresh upon theological subjects, and to
revise her opinions about the genesis of faiths, and
their influence upon morals.

In the autumn of 1846, she accepted an invitation
from her friends, Mr. and Mrs. R. V. Yates, of Liverpool, to join them in a journey to the East, they
bearing the expense. The party left England in
October; and were met at Malta by Mr. J. C. Ewart,
afterwards M.P. for Liverpool. Together, these four
travellers sailed up the Nile to the second cataract,
studied Thebes and Philæ, went up and into the Great
Pyramid, visited bazaars, mosques and (the ladies)
harems, in Cairo. Then they travelled in the track of
Moses in the desert, passing Sinai and reaching Petra.
Next, they completely traversed Palestine; and, finally,
passed through Syria to Beyrout, where they took ship
again for home. This journey occupied eight months.

In October 1847, Harriet reached "The Knoll" again,
and settled herself in her permanent course of home life.

As the same habits were continued, with only the interruptions of occasional visits to other parts of the country, day by day, for many years, I may as well mention what was the course of that daily home life.

She rose very early; not infrequently, in the winter, before daylight; and immediately set out for a good, long walk. Sometimes, I am told, she would appear at a farm-house, four miles off, before the cows were milked. The old post-mistress recollects how, when she was making up her early letter-bags, in the grey of the morning mists, Miss Martineau would come down with her large bundle of correspondence, and never failed to have a pleasant nod and smile, or a few kindly inquiries, for her humble friend. "I always go out before it is quite light," writes Miss Martineau to Mr. Atkinson, in November 1847 ; " and in the fine mornings I go up the hill behind the church—the Kirkstone road—where I reach a great height, and see from half way along Windermere to Rydal. When the little shred of moon that is left, and the morning star, hang over Wansfell, among the amber clouds of the approaching sunrise, it is delicious. On the positively rainy mornings, my walk is to Pelter Bridge and back. Sometimes it is round the south end of the valley. These early walks (I sit down to breakfast at half-past seven) are good, among other things, in preparing me in mind for my work."

Returning home, she breakfasted at half-past seven ; filled her lamp, ready for the evening, and arranged all household matters ; and by half-past eight was at her desk, where she worked undisturbed till two, the early dinner-time. These business hours were sacred, whether there were visitors in the house or not. After

dinner, however, she devoted herself to guests, if there
were any; if not, she took another walk, or, in bad
weather, did wool-work—"many a square yard of
which," she says, she "all invisibly embossed with
thoughts and feelings worked in." Tea and the newspaper came together, after which she either read, wrote
letters, or conversed for the rest of the evening, end-
ing her day always, whatever the weather, by a few
moments of silent meditation in the porch or on the
terrace without.

She was not one of those mistresses who cannot
talk to their servants, any more than she was one to
indulge them in idle and familiar gossip. If there
were any special news of the day, she would invite the
maids into her sitting-room for half an hour in the
evening, to tell them about it. During the Crimean
War, and again during the American struggle, in particular, the servants had the frequent privilege of tracing with her on the map the position of the battles,
and learning with her aid to understand the great
questions that were at stake.

The servants thus trained and considered* were not,
certainly, common domestics. She kept two girls in
the house, besides the labouring man and his wife at
the cottage; and, as the place was small, and her way
of living simple, the work did not require that she
should choose rough women for servants merely because
of their strength. On the contrary, she made special
efforts to secure young girls of a somewhat superior

* Henry Crabbe Robinson writes to Miss Fenwick on January 15,
1849 :—

"Miss Martineau makes herself an object of envy by the success
of her domestic arrangements. . . . Mrs. Wordsworth declares she
is a model in her household economy, making her servants happy,
and setting an example of activity to her neighbours."

order, whom she might train and attach to herself.
She got servants whom she had to dismiss now and
again, of course; but the time that most of her maids
stopped with her and the warm feelings that they
showed towards her, are a high testimony to the
domestic character of their " strong-minded " mistress.
At the time of which we are now speaking, her maids
were " Jane," who had been cured from chronic illness
by Miss Martineau's mesmerising, and who was in her
service for seven years, when the girl emigrated; and
" Martha," who had been trained for teaching, and
had to resign it from ill-health, but who later on
married the master of Miss Carpenter's Bristol Ragged
Schools, and returned to teaching, after serving Miss
Martineau for some eight years. Of the servants who
came after this, " Caroline " was there twenty years,
till she was removed by death; and " Mary Anne "
served Miss Martineau eleven years, till the mistress's
death closed the long term of attendance and almost
filial love.

Indications of how different the relationship was in
this home from what it only too often is, are found in
many of Miss Martineau's letters. When " Martha "
married, she had the rare honour of having Harriet
Martineau and Mary Carpenter for her bridesmaids.
The mistress gave the wedding breakfast, and partook
of it, too, in company with the bride and bridegroom
and their friends; and when she had seen them all off, she
sat down to write to her family about her loss " with
a bursting heart." References to her feelings for her
" dear friend, Caroline," will be seen presently in her
letters to Mr. Atkinson; and her care and affection for
this valued servant are expressed yet more frequently, in
letters which I may not quote, to more domestic friends.

As to " Mary Anne," she has travelled a long way while in delicate health, to see me, to tell me all she could of her mistress, and to express how glad she was "to know of anything being done to make Miss Martineau's goodness better understood." " Mary Anne " is now a married woman. She was engaged for three or four years before Miss Martineau's death, but would not leave her mistress in her old age and her ill-health. That mistress, on her part, when told of the engagement, not only admitted the lover to an interview with herself, but even generously urged that the wedding should not be delayed for her sake, although at this time she had an almost morbid shrinking from strangers, and the loss of the personal attendant who knew her ways would have been one of the greatest calamities of the commoner order that could have befallen her. But " Mary Anne " did not leave her ; and when, at last, it became quite certain that death was at hand, the generous lady said to a relative that it made her "so glad to think that, when it was over, there could be nothing to stand in the way of Mary Anne's marriage." I have thus anticipated in order to show that the domestic peace which existed under her household rule was no special thing dependent upon the character of a single servant, but was maintained through all the years of her home life, and therefore unquestionably was the result of the mistress's qualities of heart and mind.

What may be called her external home life—that is to say, what she was to her poorer neighbours—during that ten years of activity, may also be best noticed before the mental progress and literary work of the period come under further review.

Every winter, for several years, she gave a course of

lectures to the working-people and tradesfolk of the
place, in the Methodist school-room at the back of her
house. Many of the gentry desired to attend, but she
would have none of them, on the double ground that
there was no room for them, and that the lectures
were designed for people who had little access to books
or other educational resources. The subjects that she
treated were as various as those of her books, but all
chosen with what I have previously observed seems
to me to have been the object of all her works—to
influence conduct through knowledge and reasoning.
There was a course on sanitary matters, others on her
travels (and we know from her books on the same
topics from what point of view these were treated),
some on the history of England, another on the history
and constitution of the United States ; and, finally,
the last course for which she had health and strength
was given in November and December 1854, and was
on the Crimean War and the character of the govern·
ment of Russia.

I have seen some of the older inhabitants of Ambleside who attended these lectures, and who now speak
of them in the warmest terms of admiration. "They
were so clear; and she never stopped for a word ; and
so interesting !—one could have listened to them over
and over again," But there is no one who could tell,
with the aid of a cultivated taste, what she was as a
public speaker. So eloquent is some of her writing
that one holds one's breath as one reads it ; and the
evident rapidity of the penmanship of her MS.* shows

* In speaking of her eloquent writings I refer specially to the
*History of the Peace*; and I have seen the manuscript of this,
bearing evidence that the hand could not keep pace with the flow
of words and thoughts.

that such passages were produced with all the impro-
visatory impulse and flow of the orator. If, besides
this, her delivery was fervent and impressive, one cannot but think how great a statesman and parliamentary
leader she might have been, with these essential quali-
fications for modern public life added to all that knowledge, judgment, strength of principle, and political
capacity which made men willing (as we shall see soon)
to accept her as their political teacher in the daily and
quarterly press. That she had the orator's stirring
gifts, the personal magnetism which compels the minds
of a mass to move with the words of a speaker, and
the reciprocal power of receiving stimulus from an
audience, when

> The heart of many fires the lips of one,

there is one shadowy incident left to show, besides the
testimony of her local hearers who survive. It is
this : in 1849 Charlotte Brontë, then in the first flush
of her fame, sought Harriet Martineau's acquaintance,
saying that she desired "to see one whose works have
so often made her the subject of my thoughts." In
the following year Charlotte visited Harriet at "The
Knoll," and heard one of the English History lectures.
Her bright eyes were fixed on the lecturer all through ;
and as Harriet stood on her low platform, while the
audience dispersed, she heard Charlotte say, in the very
voice of the lecturer, what Edward said in the wind-
mill at Cressy : " Is my son dead ? " They walked
silently to the house together—about three hundred
paces—and when Harriet turned up her lamp in the
drawing-room, the first thing she saw was Charlotte
looking at her with wide, shining eyes, and repeating,
in the same tone, " Is my son dead ? " To those who

know the dramatic quality of Charlotte Brontë's imagination, there is a beam of light reflected from this trifling anecdote upon the force and the manner of the speaker who had so impressed her.

The opinion which this keenly observant and candid woman formed of Harriet Martineau is of peculiar interest, and, as it specially refers to the period and the relations of which we are now treating, I quote it from Mrs. Gaskell's *Life of Charlotte Brontë*. It is given in some private letters, written from " The Knoll " (not, as Mrs. Chapman absurdly says, to Emily Brontë, who was dead, but) to Charlotte's life-long and most confidential friend, Miss Ellen Nussey :—

"I am at Miss Martineau's for a week. Her house is very pleasant both within and without; arranged at all points with admirable neatness and comfort. Her visitors enjoy the most perfect liberty; what she claims for herself she allows them. . . . She is a great and good woman. . . . The manner in which she combines the highest mental culture with the nicest discharge of feminine duties filled me with admiration; while her affectionate kindness earned my gratitude. I think her good and noble qualities far outweigh her defects. It is my habit to consider the individual apart from his (or her) reputation, practice independent of theory, natural disposition isolated from acquired opinion. Harriet Martineau's person, practice, and character inspire me with the truest affection and respect.

"I find a worth and greatness in herself, and a consistency and benevolence and perseverance in her practice, such as win the sincerest esteem and affection. She is not a person to be judged by her writings alone, but rather by her own deeds and life, than which nothing can be more exemplary or nobler. She seems to me the benefactress of Ambleside, yet takes no sort of credit to herself for her active and indefatigable philanthropy. The government of her household is admirably administered; all she does is well done, from the writing of a history down to the quietest feminine occupation. No sort of carelessness or neglect is allowed under her rule, and yet she is not over-strict, or too rigidly exacting; her servants and her poor neighbours love as well as respect her.

"I must not, however, fall into the error of talking too much about her, merely because my mind is just now deeply impressed with what I have seen of her intellectual power and moral worth."

Some of her lectures were given with the express object of inducing the people to form a building society. Rents were excessively high for the working classes from the scarcity of cottages; and therefore they lived and slept crowded together, while the open country extended all around them. The moral screw was turned upon them, too, about politics and religion, by the threat of the landlord that, if they offended him, he would turn them out of the only cottages they could get. With that true philanthropy which her studies in political economy had taught, Miss Martineau went to work to aid the people to improve their own condition. She obtained a loan of £500 from her old friend, Mrs. Reid, of London (to whom the foundation of Bedford College is mainly due), with which she purchased a field just above the village at Ellercross, and parcelled it out, drained it, and made the road. Then, by her lectures, she showed the people how they could "buy a house with its rent"; and she undertook all the infinite trouble that devolved upon her when the society was formed, as the only member of it with legal and general knowledge, and, therefore, the only one able to guide its affairs. Before me there lies a package of the notes that she sent at different times on this business to Mr. Bell, the Ambleside chemist, who was the nominal chairman—though she was the real one—of the society. "Jealousy and ridicule went to work against the scheme"; but her philanthropic energy and wisdom were fully successful. The cottages are healthily planned and well built, and remain there as a monument to the efforts which she made for the good of her poor neighbours.

Besides these more general undertakings for their benefit, there yet live many amongst them who are grateful to her for personal kindness and assistance. While her strength lasted, she was ever ready to try to relieve others from illness by the means which she believed to have cured herself ; and seven mesmerised patients were sometimes asleep at one time in her drawing-room. She was a powerful mesmerist. Most of her patients were, at least, relieved—some cured. A present resident of Ambleside, who owes his success in business life to her kindness, told me how she mesmerised him for nearly an hour every day for a year; and to show that she did not do this without very decided results to herself, he remembers that her fingers used to swell during the process, so as to almost hide her rings, if she forgot to take them off before beginning.

Again, her library was placed freely at the service of deserving young men in the village—and only book-lovers will be able to appreciate the generosity of this neighbourly kindness. Old Miss Nicholson tells me of Miss Martineau's kindness to her invalid sister ; sharing with her the luxuries which were not to be bought in Ambleside, but which the famous writer frequently received from some of her many friends. Nor was the mere personal human sympathy wanting in her ; those who needed no gifts or material aid from her knew her as a kind friend, ready to think for them and advise with them in their troubles or perplexities.

In mentioning her activities other than literary, during those ten busy and healthy years of home life,

I must not omit her "farming"—her farm of two
acres. She had no intention, at first, of embarking
in such an enterprise. She let on hire that portion of
her land which she did not wish to have in her garden,
and her maids and herself, with the occasional help of
a man, kept the garden in order. But this plan did
not answer well. The tenant allowed the grass to get
untidy, and his sheep broke into the garden to eat the
cabbages. Neither the vegetable nor the flower garden
could be kept so nicely as might be wished. Milk,
butter, eggs, and hams, all had to be bought at high
prices; and so small was the supply at times that these
articles of country produce were actually unattainable
by purchase.

The energetic lady of the small domain was pro-
foundly dissatisfied with this state of affairs. So to
work she went to study the science of agriculture,
and practical farming; and soon a Norfolk labourer
was established on her land, and this small farm was
under her own management. She set up a cross-pole
fence around her estate, the first one ever seen in the
Lake District; and, like a true woman, she planted
roses all along the fence, to wreathe and decorate it in
summer. Then she initiated her fellow-farmers into
the mysteries of high farming, and stall feeding. "A
cow to three acres" was the Lake rule; but she hired
another half-acre of land, to add to her own, and
showed that upon this total of two acres she could
*almost* keep two cows. Fowls and pigs were, of course,
kept also; and all the household comforts which cows,
hens, and pigs supply were obtained from her land at,
practically, no cost at all. The subsistence of the
labourer and his wife was created out of the soil; and
the house had a constant supply of vegetables, milk,

eggs, and hams, at a less expense than buying had previously been, and with a much nicer and always certain supply.

The experiment became famous in a small way. " People came to see how we arranged our ground, so as to get such crops out of it,"* and one of the Poor-Law Commissioners, having asked her for a private account of how she had managed her little farm, printed her letter in the *Times,* without asking her consent. This brought such a flood of correspondence on her that she was compelled to write on the subject for publication, and so the farm superintendence resulted in a piece of literary work for the mistress.

Now we will see what her pen was doing while all these activities were helping to fill her days.

* *Health, Husbandry, and Handicraft,* p. 269, " Our Farm of Two Acres."

# CHAPTER IX.

## IN THE MATURITY OF HER POWERS.

THE book, published early in 1848, in which Harriet
described her Egyptian, Desert, and Palestine travels,
was entitled *Eastern Life, Past and Present.* If I were
required to give from some one only of her works a
series of extracts which should illustrate the special
powers of her mind and the finest features of her
style, it would be this book that I should choose. I
do not mean to say that the most eloquent and vivid
passage that I might find in all her writings is here ;
nor that her deepest and noblest qualities as a thinker
are more forcibly displayed here than elsewhere. But
I mean that in *Eastern Life, Past and Present,* all her
best moral and intellectual faculties were exerted, and
their action becomes visible, at one page or another,
in reading the book from the first to the last chapters.
The keen observation, the active thought, the vigorous
memory, the power of deep and sustained study, the
mastery of language, giving the ability to depict in
words and to arouse the reader's imagination to mental vision—all these requisites for the writing of a good
book of travel she showed that she possessed. But

there is even more than all this in *Eastern Life.*
There is the feeling for humanity in all its circumstances,
which can sympathise no less with the slave of the
harem at this moment alive in degradation, than with
the highest intelligences that ceased from existence
unnumbered thousands of years ago. The most interesting and characteristic feature distinguishing this
work is, however, the openness and freedom of its
thought combined with the profound reverence that it
shows for all that is venerable.

It was *Eastern Life* which first declared to the world
that Harriet Martineau had ceased to have a theology.
She had learned, in travelling through Egypt, how
much of what Moses taught was derived from the
ancient mythology of Egypt. Passing afterwards
through the lands where the Hebrew, the Christian,
and the Mohammedan faiths in turn arose, observing,
thinking, and studying, the conclusion at which she
arrived at last was, in brief, this: That men have
ever constructed the image of a Ruler of the Universe
out of their own minds; that all successive ideas about
the Supreme Power have been originated from within,
and modified by the surrounding circumstances;
and that all theologies, therefore, are baseless productions of the human imagination, and have no essential connection with those great religious ideas and
emotions by which men are constrained to live nobly,
to do justly, and to love what they see to be the true
and the right.

Her conviction that the highest moral conduct, and
the most unselfish goodness, and the noblest aspirations, are in no degree connected with any kind of
creed, was aided and supported, no doubt, by her warm
personal affection for Mr. Atkinson, and some other

of her friends of his way of thinking, in whom she
found aspirations as lofty and feelings as admirable
as ever she had enjoyed communion with, together
with a complete rejection, on scientific grounds, of all
theology.   Her belief now was that—

> The best state of mind was to be found, however it might be
> accounted for, in those who were called philosophical atheists. . . .
> I knew several of that class—some avowed, and some not; and I
> had for several years felt that they were among my most honoured
> acquaintances and friends; and now I knew them more deeply and
> thoroughly, I must say that, for conscientiousness, sincerity, in-
> tegrity, seriousness, effective intellect, *and the true religious spirit*,
> I knew nothing like them.

Her own "true religious" earnestness was unabated.
*Eastern Life* contains abundance of evidence that the
spirit in which she now wrote against all theological
systems was exactly at one with that in which she had
twenty years before written *Addresses, Prayers, and
Hymns.*   Her intellectual range had become far wider;
her knowledge of human nature and of the history and
conditions of mankind had vastly increased; but her
religious earnestness—that is to say, her devotion to
truth, and her emotional reverence for her highest
conceptions of goodness and duty—was as fervent as
ever.

Notwithstanding the boldness and heterodoxy of
*Eastern Life*, it did not cause much outcry; and her
two next books were amongst the most successful of
all her works.   The first of these was *Household Education*; the second, *A History of the Thirty Years'
Peace.*

The former was partly written for periodical publication during 1847 in the *People's Journal,* for which
magazine she wrote also a few desultory articles.

The *History of the Peace* was a voluminous work

of the first order of importance. Its execution is in most respects entirely admirable. Her task of writing the history of the time in which she had herself lived was one of extreme delicacy. Honest contemporary judgments about still-living or lately-dead persons, and about actions which have been observed with all the freshness of feeling of the passing moment, must often seem unduly stern to those who look back through the softening veil of the past, and to whom the actors have always been purely historic personages. Moreover, I have before mentioned her tendency, which seems to me to have arisen from her deafness, to give insufficient *shading off* in depicting character. But wonderfully little allowance is, after all, required on such grounds from the reader at the present day of Harriet Martineau's history of the years between 1815 and 1845. The view taken by her of O'Connell, Brougham, and some others is perhaps too stern; the picture has too many dark shades, and not a due proportion of light tints; but it can scarcely be questioned that the outline is accurate, and the whole drawing substantially correct. The earnest endeavour after impartiality, and the success with which the judicial attitude of the historian is on the whole maintained, are very remarkable.

This appears so to one who looks upon the book with the eyes of the present generation; but the recognition of the fact at the moment when she wrote is perhaps more conclusive, and the following quotation may serve to show the opinion of those who (with her) had lived through the time of which she treats.

Miss Martineau has been able to discuss events which may almost be called contemporary as calmly as if she were examining a remote period of antiquity. She has written the history of a rather undignified reign with a dignity that raises even the strifes of forgotten and exploded parties into philosophic importance. She exhibits warm sympathies for all that is noble, honourable, or exalted—and a thorough disdain of every paltry contrivance devised to serve a temporary purpose, or gain an unworthy end. The principles which she enunciates are based on eternal truths, and evolved with a logical precision that admits rhetorical ornament without becoming obscure or confused. There are few living authors who may be so implicitly trusted with the task of writing contemporary history as Miss Martineau. She has spared no pains in investigating the truth, and allowed no fears to prevent her from stating it.*

Though all her other books should die, and be buried utterly under the dust of time, this one will never be entirely lost. It is as accurate and as careful in its facts as the driest compendium, while yet its pages glow with eloquence, and are instinct with political wisdom. She really did here what she had designed to do in *Society in America*; but here she did it in the right method, there in a wrong one. The great growth of her mind in twelve years of maturity could not be better gauged than by a comparison of these two works. Her political principles did not change in the time; she was a true believer in popular government all her life—her love of justice caused her to be a hater of class rule, and of every kind of privilege; her sympathies were boundless, and made her in earnest for the freedom and progress of the democracy; her conscience was active so that she loved truth for its own sake; and her sense of duty never failed to keep alive in her large mind a feeling of personal concern in the progress of public affairs. All this was true of her when she wrote her American book; it was equally true when she treated the history of her own land and her own times. But in the latter case, she writes on

* *Athenæum*, March 31st, 1849.

political philosophy like a statesman—in the former there is much of the doctrinaire. In the latter work, principles underlie the whole fabric; but the actions of politicians are made the means of judging their own professed creeds, the value of those creeds being easily appraised by the results seen to follow on actions in conformity with them. In the earlier work, as we saw, the theories were postulated first, and the actions were measured against those self-derived standards of right and wrong. For political sagacity, for nobility of public spirit, for effective thought, for knowledge of facts, for clear presentation of them, for accuracy in judging of their permanent importance, for candour and impartiality, for insight into character, and for vivid and glowing eloquence, *The History of the Thirty Years' Peace* stands forth unmatched amongst books of its class. This, I take it, will be the most enduring and valuable of all her works, and the one by which chiefly posterity will learn what were her powers and how estimable was her character.

In the two works last mentioned, *Eastern Life* and *The Thirty Years' Peace*, it seems to me that she touched the high-water mark of her permanent achievements. We have nearly reached the end of the long catalogue of her books, though by no means the end of her writings. Very much more work she did in her life, as will presently be told; but It was that kind of work which is (with the single exception of oratory) the most powerful at the moment but the most evanescent—journalism. She was soon to begin to apply her ripe wisdom, and her life-long study of the theory of government, to the concrete problems of practical politics. The influence of an active and powerful journalist cannot be measured; the work itself cannot

be adequately surveyed and criticised ; and thus what
is, perhaps, the most useful, capable, and important
work which Harriet Martineau did, eludes our detailed
survey.  We can best judge what was her power as a
leader-writer, and review and magazine essayist, by
noting how progressively her mind improved, and to
what a high moral and intellectual standpoint she had
attained in her latest volumes, just before she exchanged
such sustained labours for the briefer though not less
arduous efforts of leading and teaching through the
periodical press.

*The History of the Peace* was completed in 1850 ; and
was so immediately successful that the publisher asked
Miss Martineau to write an introductory volume on
the history of the first fifteen years of this century.
While at work upon this " Introduction," she did also
some short articles on various subjects for Charles
Dickens's periodical, *Household Words,* and was like-
wise proceeding with the preparation of another volume
of a very different kind.  This last was published in
January, 1851 (before the introductory volume of the
*History*), under the title of *Letters on the Laws of
Man's Nature and Development,* by Henry George
Atkinson, F.G.S., and Harriet Martineau.

The contents of the book were actual letters which
had passed between the friends.  It will be remembered
that Harriet did not meet Mr. Atkinson during the
progress of her mesmeric treatment and recovery
from illness under his written advice.  But soon after
she got better, they were visiting together at the house
of a cousin of hers ; and during the six years or so
which had since then passed, they had often met, and
their correspondence had grown to be very frequent.
Mr. Atkinson had gradually become the friend dearest

to Harriet Martineau in all the world. He gained
her affection (I use the word advisedly) by entirely
honourable roads—by the delight which she took
in observing his scientific knowledge, his originality
of thought, and his elevated tone of mind. But I
cannot doubt that long before this volume of *Letters*
was published, he had become dear to her by virtue
of that personal attraction which is not altogether
dependent upon merit, but which enhances such merits
as may be possessed by the object of the attachment,
and somewhat confuses the relationship on the intellectual side. This condition of things is in no way
especially feminine : John Stuart Mill bowed down
to Mrs. Taylor, and Comte erected his admiration of
Clotilde into a *culte*. Mr. Atkinson was many years
younger than his friend, and very likely she never
fully realised the depth of her own feelings towards
him. But still the attraction had its influence, though
unacknowledged in words, and unreciprocated in kind.

Miss Martineau was really taught by Mr. Atkinson
much of science that she had not previously studied ;
but yet it was an error, from every point of view, for
her to present to the world a book in which she avowed
herself his pupil. Her letters are mainly composed
of questions, upon which she seeks enlightenment.
The answers cannot, in the nature of the case, give
forth a connected system of thought upon " Man's
Nature and Development." No one was more ready
than she herself to recognise that, as she says, " in
literature, no mind can work well upon the lines laid
down by another " ; yet this was what she required
Mr. Atkinson to do in replying to her questions and
taking up her points. The errors that one would
expect are found in the results of this mistaken form ;

the facts and the inferences are neither sufficiently separated, nor properly connected; and the real value which the book had as a contribution to science and philosophy is lost sight of in the disorder. In fact, no form could be less suitable than the epistolary for such work—either for the writers to arrange and analyze what they were doing, or for the reader to see and understand what they had done. Besides this, the public had long consented to learn from Harriet Martineau; but Mr. Atkinson, though highly respected by his own circle, was not known to the general public, and it was, therefore, an error in policy for Miss Martineau to show herself sitting as a pupil at his feet, and to call on those who believed in her to believe in him as her teacher and guide. Her fine tact and long experience must have led her to perceive all this in an ordinary case; and only the personal reason of a desire to win for her friend the recognition from the public which she herself had already given him so fully in her own head and heart, could have led an experienced and able woman of letters to so blunder in her selection of the literary form of the book.

As to the substance of the *Letters*, but little need be said, because the bulk of the volume is not her writing, but Mr. Atkinson's. The ideas which she had then accepted, however, were those by which she lived the rest of her life, and must have their due share of notice for that reason.

The fundamental point in the book is its insistance on the Baconian, or experiential, or scientific, method of inquiry being adopted in studying man and his mental constitution, just as much as in studying inanimate nature. A great First Cause of all things is not denied, but declared unknown and unknowable, as necessarily beyond the comprehension of the senses of man. Supernatural revelation is, of course, entirely rejected; indeed, the very word supernatural is held to involve a fallacy, for only natural things can be known. Mr. Atkinson pointed out that the whole of the facts which are around us can be observed, analyzed, and found to occur in an invariable sequence of causes and effects, which form natural laws; and that the mind of man is no exception to this general truth that all events spring from causes, and are themselves in turn causes of other effects. It follows from these conclusions that the " First Cause " (which, as Miss Martineau said, the constitution of the human mind requires it to suppose) never intervenes in the world as an errant influence, disturbing natural law; and all speculations about its nature, character, and purposes are put aside as out of the field of inquiry.

Passing on from method to results, Mr. Atkinson gave the first hints of many doctrines now fully accepted: as that of unconscious cerebration, or that of more senses than five, for instance; and of many others (based mainly on phrenology and mesmerism) not held, up to the present time, even by the scientists of his own school. For the rest the book has much that is interesting; it has much that is true; but it has, also, much that might well have been put forward as speculation, but should not have been stated so dogmatically as it was on the evidence available.*

* It is right that I should say that I alone am responsible for the above (necessarily imperfect) digest of the contents of the book. I at first thought of asking Mr. Atkinson to do me the favour of reading my account of his work in proof; but I ultimately concluded that it would be better that in this instance, as

It was received in 1851 with a howl from the orthodox press which would seem strange indeed in these
days.  But of competent criticism it had very little.
Miss Martineau's name, of course, secured attention
for it ; and small though her share in the book was, it
was quite enough to make the fact perfectly clear that
she was henceforth to be looked upon as a " material-
ist " and a " philosophical atheist," and the rest of the
names by which it was customary to stigmatise any
person who rejected supernaturalism and revelation.

The motives with which this book was written and
published could hardly be misunderstood.  There could be
no idea of making money out of a work on philosophy
—even if either of the authors had been in the habit
of writing merely to make money; while as to fame
and applause, everyone is more or less acquainted with
the history of the reception given in all ages to those
who have questioned the popular beliefs of their time !
The sole motive with which Harriet Martineau wrote
and issued this book was the same that impelled her
to do all her work—the desire to teach that which she
believed to be true, and to be valuable in its influence
upon conduct.  With regard to the latter point, it
seemed to her that one great cause for the slow
advance of civilisation is the degree to which good
men and women have occupied themselves with supernatural concerns, neglecting for these the actual world,
its conditions, and its wants, and giving themselves
over to the guidance of a spiritual hierarchy instead
of exercising all their own powers in freedom.  She
struck at this error in publishing the *Letters*.  At the

in the case of all Harriet Martineau's other books, I myself should
be wholly responsible to the public for my own substantial accuracy
and fairness.

same time she felt doubtful if her future writings would ever be read after her bold utterances, and even, as the following letter shows, whether she might not find herself the occupant of a felon's dock for the crime of which Socrates, and Jesus, and Galileo were each in turn accused—blasphemy :

LETTER TO MR. ATKINSON.

[Extract.]                        August 10, 1874.

One thing more is worth saying. Do you remember how, when we were bringing out our "Letters," I directed your attention to our Blasphemy Law, and the trial of Moxon, under that law, for publishing Shelley's "Queen Mab" among his *Poems*? You ridiculed my statement, and said Mr. Procter * denied there being such a law, or Moxon having been tried, in the face of the fact that I had corresponded with Moxon on the occasion, on the part of certain personal friends. The fact appeared afterwards in the *Annual Register*, but it seemed to produce no effect. Well! now you can know the truth by looking at the *Life of Denman*, by Sir Joseph Arnould. If you can lay your hands on the book, please look at vol. ii. p. 129, where there is an account of the trial, Judge Denman being the judge who tried the case. The narrative ends thus :—" The verdict was for the Crown" (conviction for blasphemy), " but Mr. Moxon was never called up for sentence." It is too late for Mr. Procter to learn the truth, but it is surely always well for us, while still engaged in the work of life, to be accurately informed on such matters as the laws we live under, and our consequent responsibilities. Is it not so?

It was, then, with the full anticipation, not only of social obloquy, but also of legal penalty, that the brave thinker fulfilled (to quote her own words in the Preface to the *Letters*) " that great social duty, to impart what we believe, and what we think we have learned. Among the few things of which we can pronounce ourselves certain is the obligation of inquirers after truth to communicate what they obtain." The heroic soul fulfilled now, as before and afterwards, what she held

* " Barry Cornwall."

to be her duty, as simply and unwaveringly as ever a soldier on the battle-field charged the cannon's mouth.

Five times in her life did Harriet Martineau write and publish that which she believed would ruin her prospects, silence her voice for ever, and close her career. Far from her was that common paltering with the conscience by which so many men confuse their minds—the poor pretence that truth must not be spoken for fear that the speaker's influence for future worthy work may be injured by his boldness. This is how the devil tempts, saying, " Fall down, and worship me, and I will give thee all the kingdoms of the earth and the glory of them." Harriet Martineau never worshipped evil even by silence, when silence was sin, playing fast and loose with her conscience by a promise to use the power so obtained for higher objects hereafter. The truth that appeared to her mind she spoke frankly; the work that was placed for her to do she did simply; and so the quagmire of the expedient never engulfed her reputation, her self-respect, and her usefulness, as it has done that of so many who have been lured into it from the straight path of right action and truthful speech in public life, by will-o'-the-wisp hopes of greater power and glory for themselves in the future—which they hope they may use for good when they shall be smothered in cowardice and lies. She had much to suffer, and did suffer. Martyrs are not honoured because they are insensate, but because they defy their natural human weaknesses in maintaining that which they believe to be true. Probably the keenest grief which she experienced on the occasion now before us came from the complete separation which took place between her and the dearest friend of her youth, her brother James. Dr. Martineau was, at that time, one of the editors of the *Prospective Review.* Philosophy was his department, and in the natural order the *Letters* came to him for review. He reviewed the book accordingly, and in such terms that all intercourse between him and his sister was thenceforward at an end. They had long before drifted apart in thought; but this final separation was none the less felt as a wrench. Dr. Martineau's attack was almost exclusively aimed against Mr. Atkinson. But with Harriet's loyalty of nature she was more impelled to resent what was said about her friend and colleague than if it had been directed against herself. The brother and sister never met or communicated with each other again.

The introductory volume of the *History of the Peace* was published soon after the Atkinson *Letters.* The next work which she undertook was a great labour— the rendering into English of Comte's *Positive Philosophy.*

What she accomplished with this book was not a mere translation, nor could it be precisely described as a condensation; it was both these and more. Comte had propounded his groundwork of philosophy and his outline of all the sciences in six bulky volumes, full of repetitions, and written in an imperfect French style. Harriet Martineau rendered the whole substance of these six volumes into two of clear English, orderly, consecutive, and scientific in method as in substance. So well was her work accomplished that Comte himself adopted it for his students' use, removing from his list of books for Positivists his own edition of his course, and recommending instead the English version by Miss Martineau. It thus by-and-bye came to pass that

Comte's own work fell entirely out of use, and his complete teachings became inaccessible to the French people in their own tongue; so that twenty years afterwards, when one of his disciples wished to call public attention to the master's work as teaching the method of social science by which the French nation must find its way back to prosperity after the great war, he was constrained to ask Harriet Martineau's permission to re-translate her version.

Comte wrote her the warmest expressions of his gratitude; but this he owed her on another ground besides the one of the value of her labours in popularising his work so ably. While she was labouring at her task, Mr. Lombe, then High Sheriff of Norfolk, sent her a cheque for £500, which he begged her to accept, since she was doing a work which he had long desired to see accomplished, but which he knew could not possibly be remunerative to her. She accepted the money, but, with her customary generosity in pecuniary affairs, she employed more than half of it in paying the whole expenses of publication, and arranged that the proceeds of the sale, whatever they might be, should be shared with M. Comte.

There was a considerable demand for the work on its first appearance; and up to this present date a fair number of copies is annually disposed of. It came out in November 1853, having partly occupied her time during the preceding two years. Only partly, however; for, besides all the efforts for her neighbourhood previously referred to (the building society was in progress during those years, and gave her much thought, as her business notes are in evidence), and besides her farming, she was now writing largely for periodicals and newspapers. These are the pulpits from which

our modern preachers are most widely and effectively
heard, and the right tone of which is, therefore, of
the first consequence to society. For every hundred
persons who listen to the priest, the journalist (including in this term writers for all periodicals) speaks
to a thousand; and while the words of the one are
often heard merely as a formality, those of the other,
dealing with the matters at the moment most near and
interesting to his audience, may effectively influence
the thoughts and consciences and actions of thousands
in the near future. Shallow, indeed, would be the
mind which undervalued the power of the journalist,
or underrated the seriousness of his vocation. Harriet
Martineau saw the scope which journalism afforded for
the kind of work which she had all her life been doing
—the influencing of conduct by considering practical
affairs in the light of principle. Her periodical writing
being, according to our mistaken English custom,
anonymous, neither brought her any increase of fame
nor carried with it the influence which her personality
as a teacher would have contributed to the weight of
what she wrote. Nevertheless, she repeatedly, in her
letters, speaks of her journalism as the most delightful
work of her life, and that which she believed had been
perhaps the most useful of all her efforts.

Some stories with sanitary morals, which she now
contributed to *Household Words*, were admirably
written. "The People of Bleaburn" is the true
story of what was done by a grand American woman,
Mary Ware, when she happened to go into an isolated
village at the very time that half its inhabitants were
lying stricken down by an epidemic. "Woodruffe,
the Gardener," was a presentation of the evils of living
in low-lying, damp countries. "The Marsh Fog and

the Sea Breeze" is perhaps the most interesting of all her stories since the Political Economy tales, which it much resembles in lightness of touch and in practical utility.

A series of slight stories under the general title of "Sketches from Life," was also contributed at this time to the *Leader*; they were all of them true tales and, like most real life stories, extremely pathetic. The most touching is one called "The Old Governess," describing the feelings with which an educated elderly woman, past her work, and with an injured hand, sought refuge in the workhouse; and how she conducted herself there. These stories were republished in a volume in 1856.

A series of descriptive accounts of manufactures, some of which contain most graphic writing, were also done in this time. These papers, with others written between 1845–55, were republished in a volume in 1861.* There are some passages which I am greatly tempted to quote, merely as specimens of the perfection to which her literary style had at this time arrived. It is now a style of that clear simplicity which seems so easy to the reader, but which is in reality the highest triumph of the literary artist. The inexperienced reader is apt to suppose that anybody could write thus, until perhaps he gains some glimpse of the truth by finding the powerful effect which it is producing upon his thoughts and imagination. The practised writer knows meanwhile that, simple though the vocabulary appears, he could not change a word for the better; and easily though the sentences swing, the rounding of their rhythm is an achievement to admire. I may not pause to quote, but I may specially refer to the

* *Health, Husbandry, and Handicraft.*

paper on " The Life of a Salmon," in illustration of this
eloquence of style.

Early in 1852, Harrriet Martineau received an invitation from the *Daily News* to send a " leader" occasionally. Busily engaged as she was with Comte, and
with work for other periodicals, she yet gladly accepted
this proposition; and thus began her connection with
that paper (then newly started) which was so valuable
both to her and the proprietors of the *Daily News*.
During the early summer of 1852, she wrote two
" leaders " each week, and, before she had finished
Comte, the regular contributions to the newspaper had
grown to three a week.

In the autumn of 1852 she made a two months'
tour through Ireland; and at the request of the editor
she wrote thence a descriptive letter for publication
in the *Daily News*, almost every other day. The
letters described the state of Ireland at the moment,
with observations such as few were so well qualified as
she to make upon the facts. She did now what
Daniel O'Connell had entreated her to do years before.
In 1839 the Liberator begged her to travel through
his country, and without bias or favour represent calmly
what really was the political and social condition of
Ireland.* The " Letters from Ireland " attracted immediate attention as they appeared in the *Daily News*;
and before the end of the year they were republished
in a volume. At the same time some of her " leaders "
secured much attention, and the editor pressed her to

* It may be mentioned that a similar plea was made to her by
the Crown Prince Oscar of Sweden, who desired her aid in preparing his people for constitutional reform; and again, at a later
date, by Count Porro, of Milan, who begged that she would let
the world know what was the condition of Italy under Austrian rule.

write even more frequently. During 1853 she wrote on an average four articles a week, and shortly afterwards the number rose to six—one in each day's paper.

The tale of the journalistic work of these busy two years is not yet complete. There is a long article of hers in the *Westminster Review* for January, 1853; the subject is, "The Condition and Prospects of Ireland."

All this journalism was done at the same time that the heavy sustained task of the condensation of Comte's abstruse and bulky work was proceeding. When to all this we add in our recollection her home duties, and when the fact is borne in mind that it was her common practice to take immense walks, not infrequently covering from twelve to fifteen miles in the day, it will be seen that the mere industry and energy that she showed were most extraordinary. But, besides this, her work was of a high order of literary excellence, and full of intellectual power.

Such incessant labour is not to be held up as altogether an example to be imitated. There are some few whose duty it is to consciously moderate the amount of labour to which their mental activity impels them ; and no one ought to allow the imperative brain to overtax the rest of the system. During the Irish journey, Harriet began to be aware of experiencing unusual fatigue. She gave herself no sufficient pause, however, either then or afterwards, until she could not help doing so.

After the publication of Comte she wrote a remarkable article for the *Westminster Review* (anonymous of course), on "England's Foreign Policy." This appeared in the number for January, 1854. It dealt largely with the impending struggle between England

and Russia. True Liberal as Harriet Martineau was, she hated with all her soul—not the Russian people, but—the hideous despotism, the Asiatic, and barbarian, and brutal Government of that Empire. She foresaw a probable great struggle in the future between tyranny and freedom, in which Russia, by virtue of all her circumstances, will be the Power against which the free peoples of the earth will have to fight. Not only, then, did she fully recognise the necessity for the immediate resistance, which the Crimean War was, to the encroachments on Europe of the Czar, but her article also included a powerful plea for the abolition of that system of secrecy of English diplomacy, by which it is rendered quite possible for our Ministry to covertly injure our liberties, and to take action behind our backs in our names in opposition to our warmest wishes. The article, as a whole, is one of her most powerful pieces of writing; and had it been delivered as a speech in Parliament it would undoubtedly have produced a great effect, and have placed her high amongst the statesmen of that critical time.

In the April (1854) number of the same Review, there appeared an article from her pen upon "The Census of 1851." This paper was not a mere comment upon the census return, but an historical review of the progress of the English people from barbarism to the civilisation of our century.

In the spring of this year she made a careful survey of the beautiful district around her home, in order to write a *Complete Guide to the Lakes* for a local publisher. She was already thoroughly acquainted with the neighbourhood, by means of her long and frequent predestrian excursions, and reminiscences of these abound in this " Guide." The vivid description

of a storm on Blake Fell, for instance, is a faithful
account of an occurrence during a visit which a niece
and nephew from Birmingham paid to her soon after
her settlement at the Lakes. The word-paintings of
the scenery, too, were drawn not from what she saw
on one set visit only, but were the results of her many
and frequent pilgrimages to those beauties of nature
which she so highly appreciated. But still she would
not write her " Guide" without revisiting the whole
of the district.

The most interesting point about this book is that
it reveals one feature of her character that all who
knew her mention, but that very rarely appears in her
writings. This is, her keen sense of humour. She
dearly loved a good story, and could tell one herself
with pith and point. Her laugh is said to have been
very hearty and ready. Even when she was old and
ill, she was always amusable, and her laughter at any
little bit of fun would even then ring through her
house as gaily as though the outburst had been that
of a child's frank merriment. It is surprising that
this sense of, and enjoyment in, the ludicrous so rarely
appears in her writings. But I think it was because
her authorship was to her too serious a vocation for
fun to come into it often. She felt it almost as the
exercise of a priestly function ; it was earnest and
almost solemn work for her to write what might be
multiplied through the printing-press many thousand
times over, and so uttered to all who had ears to hear.
She showed that this was so by the greater deliberate-
ness with which she expressed judgments of persons
and pronounced opinions of any kind in her writings
than in conversation. Similarly she showed it by the
abeyance of her humour in writing ; it was no more

possible for her to crack jokes when seated at her desk than it would have been for a priestess when standing by her tripod. But this particular book, this " Guide, written for neighbourly reasons," did not admit of the seriousness of her intellect being called into action, and the result is that it is full of good stories and lighted up with fun. Her enjoyment in such stories reveals that sense of humour which, however strongly visible in daily intercourse, rarely appears in her books in any other form than in her perfect appreciation of the line between the sublime and the ludicrous.

This summer brought her much annoyance of a pecuniary kind. Her generosity about money matters was repeatedly shown, from the time when she left her " Illustrations " in the hands of Mr. C. Fox, onwards; and she had now given what was for her means an extravagant contribution to the maintenance of the *Westminster Review,* taking a mortgage on the proprietorship for her only security. In the summer of 1854, Dr. Chapman, its publisher and editor, failed; and an attempt was made to upset the mortgage. Harriet Martineau gave Chapman the most kindly assistance and sympathy in his affairs at this juncture; not only overlooking the probable loss to herself, but exerting herself to write two long articles for the next number of the Review (October 1854).

One of these essays is on " Rajah Brooke "; a name that has half faded out of the knowledge of the present generation, but which well deserves memory for the heroic devotedness, and courage, and governing faculty of the man. His qualities were those most congenial to Harriet Martineau; and, finding his enemies active and potent, she made a complete study of his case, and represented it in full in an article, which (like her previous one on " Foreign Policy"), was so statesman-like and so wise, so calm and yet so eloquent, that it would have made her famous amongst the politicians of the day had it been delivered as a speech in the House, instead of being printed anonymously in a Review with too small a circulation to pay its way.

Nor did her generous aid to Dr. Chapman end here. He was disappointed of some expected contributions, and Miss Martineau wrote him a second long article for the same number—the one on " The Crystal Palace," which concludes the *Westminster* for October 1854. Her two contributions amounted to fifty-four pages of print—truly a generous gift to an impecunious magazine editor.

It was now precisely ten years since her recovery from her long illness. The work done in that time shows how complete the recovery had been. Those ten happy years of vigour and of labour were, she was wont to say, Mr. Atkinson's gift to her. Well had she used these last years of her strength.

# CHAPTER X.

### IN RETREAT : JOURNALISM.

MISS MARTINEAU's health failed towards the end of
1854; and early in 1855 symptoms of a disorganised
circulation became so serious that she went up to
London to consult physicians. Dr. Latham and Sir
Thomas Watson both came to the conclusion that
she was suffering from enlargement and enfeeble-
ment of the heart; and, in accordance with her wish
to hear a candid statement of her case, they told her
that her life would probably not be much prolonged.
In short, they gave her to understand that she was
dying; and her own sensations confirmed the impressions. She had frequent sinking fits; and every night,
when she lay down, a struggle for breath began, which
lasted sometimes for hours. She received her death
sentence then, and began a course of life as trying to
the nerves and as searching a test of character as could
well be imagined. That trial she bore nobly for
twenty-one long, suffering years.

She was carefully carried home, and at once occupied herself with making every preparation for the
departure from earth which she supposed to be im-

pending.   The first business was to make a new Will;
and this was a characteristic document.   After ordering that her funeral should be conducted in the
plainest manner, and at the least possible cost, she
continued thus :—" It is my desire, from an interest
in the progress of scientific investigation, that my
skull should be given to Henry George Atkinson, of
Upper Gloucester Place, and also my brain, if my death
take place within such distance of the said Henry
George Atkinson's then present abode as to enable
him to have it for purposes of scientific investigation."
Her property was then ordered to bear various small
charges, including one of £200 to Mrs. Chapman for
writing a conclusion to the testator's autobiography,
over and above a fourth share of the profits on the
sale of the whole work after the first edition.   "The
Knoll" was bequeathed to her favourite " little sister,"
Ellen.   The remainder of her possessions were divided
amongst all her brothers and sisters, or their heirs,
with as much impartiality as though she held, with
Maggie Tulliver's aunt Glegg, that " in the matter of
wills, personal qualities were subordinate to the great
fundamental fact of blood."   Although mesmerism
had estranged her from a sister, and theology from a
brother, she made no display of bitter feeling towards
them and theirs in her last will.

All her personal affairs being made as orderly as
possible, she proceeded to write her autobiography.
Readers of that interesting but misleading work must
bear in mind that it was a very hasty production.   The
two large volumes were written in a few months; the
MS. was sent to the printer as it was produced,
the sheets for the first edition were printed off, then the
matter was stereotyped, and the sheets and plates were

packed up in the office of the printer, duly insured, and held ready for immediate publication after her death. She wrote in this hot haste with " the shadow cloaked from head to foot" at her right hand. So much reason had she to believe that her very days were numbered, that she wrote the latter part of her " autobiography " before the first portion. She had already given forth, in *Household Education* and *The Crofton Boys*, the results of her childish experiences of life ; and she was now specially anxious not to die without leaving behind her a definite account of the later course of her intellectual history.

No one who knew her considers that she did herself justice in the *Autobiography*. It is hard and cen- sorious ; it displays vanity, both in its depreciation of her own work, and in its recital of the petty slights and insults which had been offered to her from time to time ; it is aggressive, as though replying to enemies rather than appealing to friends ; and no one of either the finer or the softer qualities of her nature is at all adequately indicated. It is, in short, the least worthy of her true self of all the writings of her life.

The reasons for this unfortunate fact are not far to seck. Her rationalism, and the abuse and moral ill-usage which she had incurred by her avowal of her anti-theological opinions, were still new to her. Her very thoughts, replacing as they did the ideas which she had held without examination for some twenty years (the time which intervened between her devo- tional writings and her *Eastern Life*) were still so far new that they had not the unconsciousness and the quiet placidity which habit alone gives ; for new ideas, like new clothes, sit uneasily, and are noticeable to their wearer, however carefully they may have been fitted before adoption. Again, the announcement in the press that her illness was fatal revived the discussion of her infidelity, and brought down upon her a whole avalanche of signed and anonymous letters, of little tracts, awe-inspiring hymns, and manuals of divinity. The letters were controversial, admonishing, minatory, or entreating; but whatever their character they were all agreed upon one point, viz. that her unbelief in Christianity was a frightful sin, of which she had been wilfully guilty. They all agreed in supposing that it was within her own volition to resume her previous faith, and that she would not only go to eternal perdition if she did not put on again her old beliefs, but that she would richly deserve to do so for her wilful wickedness.

Thus, as Miss Arnold remarked to me, the moment at which she wrote the autobiography was the most aggressive and unpleasant of her whole life. Conscious as she was of the purity of her motives in uttering her philosophical opinions, she found herself suddenly spoken to by a multitude, whom she could not but know were mentally and morally incapable of judging her, as a sinner, worthy of their pity and reprobation. Knowing that she had long been recognised as a teacher, in advance of the mass of society in knowledge and power of thought, here was a crowd of people talking to her in the tones which they might have adopted towards some ignorant inmate of a prison. What wonder that her wounded self-esteem seemed for a little while to pass into vanity, when she had to remind the world, from which such insults were pouring in, of all that she had done for its instruction in the past? What wonder that the strength which was summoned up to bear with fortitude this species of modern martyrdom, seemed to give a tone of coldness and hardness to writing of so personal a kind? Then the extreme haste with which the writing and printing were done gave no time for the subsidence of such painful impressions ; and great physical suffering and weakness, together with the powerful depressing medicines which were being employed, added to the difficulty of writing with calmness, and with a full possession ot the sufferer's whole nature. In short, an autobiography could not have been written under less favourable conditions. All things taken into account, it is no wonder that those who knew and loved her whole personality are shocked and amazed at the inadequate presentation given of it in those volumes. The sensitive, unselfish, loving, domestic woman, and the just, careful, disinterested, conscientious and logical author, were alike obscured rather than revealed ; and the biographer whom she chose to complete the work had neither the intimate personal knowledge, the mental faculty which might have supplied its place, nor the literary skill requisite to present a truer picture.

Her *Autobiography* completed, the plates engraved, and all publishing arrangements made, she might, had she been an ordinary invalid, have settled down into quiet after so hard-working a life. Harriet Martineau could not do this. Her labours continued uninterruptedly, and were pursued to the utmost limit which her illness would allow. She did not cease (except during the few months that the autobiography was in hand) writing her "leaders" for the *Daily News*. Every week it contained articles by her, instructing thousands of readers. Yet she was *very* ill. She never left her home again, after that journey to London early in 1855. Sometimes she was well enough to go

out upon her terrace; and she frequently sat in her
porch, which was a bower, in the summer time, of
clematis, honeysuckle, and passion-flowers, intermingled
with ivy; but she could do no more. She was given,
as soon as she became ill, the daughterly care of her
niece, Maria, the daughter of her elder brother, Robert
Martineau, of Birmingham; and no mother ever received tenderer care or more valuable assistance from
her own child than Harriet Martineau did from the
sensible and affectionate girl whose life was thenceforth
devoted to her service. Maria once tried if her aunt
could be taken out of her own grounds in a bath-
chair: but before they reached the gates a fainting fit
came on, with such appalling symptoms of stoppage
of the heart that the experiment was never repeated.
Sometimes Miss Martineau would be well enough to
see visitors; more frequently, however, those whom
she would most have liked to talk with had to be sent
away by the doctor's orders. But, through it all, her
work continued.

Soon after the *Autobiography* was finished, she wrote
a long paper upon a most important subject, and one
which she felt to be a source of the gravest anxiety
for the future of English politics—the true sphere of
State interference with daily life. The common ignorance and carelessness upon this point she believed to
be the most painful and perilous feature of our present
situation.

It has been brought to light by beneficent action which is, in
another view, altogether encouraging. Our benevolence towards
the helpless, and our interest in personal morality, have grown
into a sort of public pursuit; and they have taken such a hold on
us that we may fairly hope that the wretched and the wronged
will never more be thrust out of sight. But, in the pursuit of our
new objects, we have fallen back—far further than 1688—in the

principle of our legislative proposals—undertaking to provide by law against personal vices, and certain special social contracts.

Her devotion to freedom, and her belief in personal liberty, led her to write an article on " Meddlesome Legislation " for the *Westminster Review*.

Her pecuniary sacrifices for the *Review* had been made because she looked upon it as an organ for free speech. Her feelings may be imagined when the editor refused to insert this article, not on any ground of principle, but merely because it spoke too freely of some of the advocates of meddlesome factory laws. The essay was published, however, as a pamphlet, and had such influence upon a Bill then before Parliament that the Association of Factory Occupiers requested to be allowed to signalise their appreciation of it by giving one hundred guineas in her name to a charity. A somewhat similar piece of work followed in the next year, a rather lengthy pamphlet *On Corporate Traditions and National Rights*. She offered nothing more to the *Westminster Review*, however, for some time; not, indeed, until that subject in which she took so profound an interest, the welfare of the United States, and the progress of the Anti-Slavery cause, seemed to require of her that she should avail herself of every possible means of addressing the public upon it. Then, in 1857, she wrote an article on *The Manifest Destiny of the American Union*, which appeared in the *Westminster* for July of that year.

Having thus signalised her forgiveness of that *Review*, she went on writing again for it for a little while. In the October number of the same year there was a paper by her on *Female Dress in* 1857. Crinoline had then lately been introduced by the Empress of the French. If one good, rousing argument could have stood in

the path of fashion, this amusing and vigorous paper
from Harriet Martineau's sick room might have
answered the purpose. But, alas! crinoline flourished;
and five whole years later on was still so enormous
that she took up her parable against it once more, in
*Once a Week*, as the cause of " Wilful Murder."

About this time she determined to assume the prefix
of " Mrs." "There were so many Misses Martineau,"
she said; and, besides, she felt the absurdity of a woman
of mature years bearing only the same complimentary
title as is accorded to a little girl in short frocks at
school. Her cards, and the envelopes of her friends,
bore thenceforward the inscription, " Mrs. Harriet
Martineau."

Although she continued to write, contributing almost
every day to the *Daily News*, as well as to these larger
periodicals, she was, it must be remembered, an invalid.
Her health fluctuated from day to day ; but it may as
well be explicitly stated that she was more or less ill
during the whole of the rest of her life. She suffered
a considerable amount daily of actual pain, which was
partly the consequence of the medicines prescribed for
her, and partly the result of the displacement of the
internal organs arising, as her doctors led her to
suppose, from the enlargement of the heart; but in
reality, as was afterwards discovered, from the growth
of a tumour. Her most constant afflictions were the
difficulty of breathing, dizziness, and dimness of sight,
resulting from disturbed circulation. At irregular,
but not infrequent, intervals she was seized with
fainting-fits, in which her heart appeared to entirely
cease beating for a minute or two; and it was not
certain from day to day but that she might die in one
of these attacks.

Not only did she continue her work under these conditions, but her interest in her poor neighbours remained unabated. There is more than one man now living in Ambleside who traces a part of his prosperity to the interest which she from her sick room displayed in his progress. A photograph of her, still sold in Ambleside, was taken in her own drawing-room by a young beginner whom she allowed thus to benefit himself. He and several others were given free access to her library. A sickly young woman in the village was made a regular sharer in the good things—the wine, the turtle soup, the game, and the flowers—which devoted friends sent frequently to cheer Harriet Martineau's retirement. Every Christmas, there was a party of the oldest inhabitants of Ambleside invited, to spend a long day in the kitchen of "The Knoll." The residents in her own cottages looked upon her less as a landlady than as a friend to whom to send in every difficulty.

Nor did she cease to do whatever was possible to her in the local public life. The question of Church Rates was approaching a crisis when she was taken ill; and when the Ambleside Quakers resolved to organize resistance to payment of these rates, they found Harriet Martineau ready to help. The householders who refused to pay were summoned before the local bench, and it was Harriet Martineau whom the justices selected to be distrained upon; but events marched rapidly, and the distraint was not made.

The next article that she contributed to the *Westminster Review* appeared in the July 1858 number, and, under the title of *The Last Days of Church Rates*, gave an account of the efforts by which Nonconformists in all parts of the country were rendering this impost impossible.

In October 1858, there was another long article in the *Westminster*, entitled *Travel during the Last Half-Century.* She was now, however, growing tired of wasting her work in that quarter, and, as we shall presently see, she sought a more influential and appreciative medium for her longer communications with the public.

Subjects which could be treated briefly were always taken up as "leaders" for the *Daily News*. Lengthier topics, too, were occasionally dealt with in those columns in the form of serial articles. One set of papers on *The Endowed Schools of Ireland*, were contributed in this manner, in 1857, to the *Daily News*, and afterwards reprinted in a small volume. In that same year occurred the terrible Indian crisis which compelled the people of this country to give, for a time, the attention which they so begrudge to their great dependency. Mrs. Martineau then wrote a series of articles, under the title of *The History of British Rule in India*, for the *Daily News*, and this most useful work was immediately republished in a volume. Alas! even she could not make so involved and distant a story interesting; but her book was clear and vivid, and whenever it dealt with the practical problem of the moment, it was full of wisdom and conscientiousness. This volume was immediately followed by *Suggestions towards the Future Government of India.* The preface of the first is dated October 1857; and that of the second, January 1858. The key-note of these books is a plea for the government of India according to Indian ideas; and, as a natural consequence, its government with the assistance of its natives. Courage as well as insight were required at *that* particular moment of popular passion to put forward these calm, statesman-like ideas. The wisdom and the practical value of the books cannot be shown by extracts; but one paragraph may be given as a faint indication of the tone:—" If instead of attempting to hold India as a preserve of English destinies, a nursery of British fortunes, we throw it open with the aim of developing India for the Indians, by means of British knowledge and equity, we shall find our own highest advantage, political and material, and may possibly recognise brethren and comrades at length, where we have hitherto perceived only savages, innocents, or foes."* Such was the spirit to which the *Daily News,* under Harriet Martineau's hand, led the people at a moment of great political excitement. The amplest testimony to the practical wisdom of the suggestions that she made was borne by those Anglo-Indians who were qualified to judge.

In June 1858, she wrote the first letter, which lies before me, to her relative, Mr. Henry Reeve, the editor of the *Edinburgh Review.* In this, after telling him that she never before has offered or wished to write for that *Review,* because in politics she had generally disagreed with it (to her, it may be remarked in passing, Toryism was less odious than official Whigism), she says that she has now a subject in view which she thinks would be suitable for the pages of the good old Whig organ. Before entering into details, she begs him to tell her frankly if any article will be refused merely because it comes from her. She adds that her health is so sunk and her life so pre-

* *Future Government of India,* p. 94.

carious, that all her engagements have to be made
with an explanation of the chances against their fulfil-
ment ; still she *does* write a good deal, and with higher
success than in her younger days.

Mr. Reeve replied cordially inviting her contributions, and the result was the establishment both of an
intimate correspondence with him, and of a relationship with the *Review* under his charge, which lasted
until she could write no more.

The particular subject which she offered Mr. Reeve
at first did not seem to him a suitable one. The title
of it was to have been *French Invasion Panics*; but as
Mr. Reeve did not like the idea, the paper was not
written. But for the *Edinburgh* of April 1859, she
wrote a long article *On Female Industry*, which attracted
much attention. Its purpose was to show how greatly
the conditions of women's lives are altered in this century from what they were of old. " A very large proportion of the women of England earn their own bread;
and there is no saying how much good may be done
by a timely recognition of this simple truth. A social
organization framed for a community of which half
stayed at home while the other half went out to work,
cannot answer the purposes of a society of which a
quarter remains at home while three quarters go out
to work." After considering in detail, with equal
benevolence and wisdom, the condition of the various
classes of women workers—those employed in agriculture, mines, fishing, domestic service, needle-work, and
shop-keeping, and suggesting, in passing, the schools of
cookery which have since become established facts, the
article concludes: " The tale is plain enough. So far
from our countrywomen being all maintained as a matter of fact by us, the ' bread-winners,' three millions

out of six of adult English women work for subsistence, and two out of the three in independence. With this new condition of affairs new duties and new views must be adopted. Old obstructions must be removed; and the aim must be set before us, as a nation as well as in private life, to provide for the free development and full use of the powers of every member of the community." It scarcely needs to be pointed out that here she went quietly but surely to the foundation of that whole class of new claims and demands on behalf of the women of our modern world, of which she was so valuable an advocate, and for the granting of which her life was so excellent a plea. In these few sentences she at one time displayed the character of the changes required, and the reasons why it is now necessary, as it did not use to be, that women should be completely enfranchised, industrially and otherwise.

The year 1859 was a very busy one. Besides the long article just mentioned, she published in April ot that year quite a large volume on *England and her Soldiers*. The book was written to aid the work which her beloved friend, Florence Nightingale, had in hand for the benefit of the army. It was, in effect, a popularisation of all that had come out before the Royal Commission on the Sanitary Condition of the Army; with the additional advantage ot the views and opinions of Florence Nightingale, studied at first hand. One of the most beautiful features of the book is the hearty and generous delight with which the one illustrious lady recounts the efforts, the sacrifices, and the triumphs of the other.

In 1859, also, Mrs. Martineau began to write frequent letters for publication to the American *Anti*

*Slavery Standard.* The affairs of the Republic were plainly approaching a crisis; and those in America who knew how well-informed she was on the politics of both countries, and on political principles, were anxious to have the guidance that only she could give in the difficult time that was approaching. During the three years, 1859 to 1861, she sent over ninety long articles for publication in America.

An article on *Trades Unions* denouncing the tyranny of men in fustian coats sitting round a beer-shop table, as to the full as mischievous as that of crowned and titled despots, appeared in the *Edinburgh Review* for October 1859. In the July 1860 issue of the same *Review* she wrote on *Russia,* and in the October of that year on *The American Union.*

Besides these large undertakings, she was writing during these years almost weekly articles, on one topic or another, for the illustrated periodical *Once a Week;* whilst the *Daily News* "leaders" continued without intermission during the whole time. As regards these latter, I shall presently mention when she entirely ceased to write; but in the meanwhile I do not attempt to follow them in detail. Nothing that I could say would give any adequate impression of their quality. *That* may be sufficiently judged by the fact that the newspaper in which they were issued was one of the best of the great London dailies; and that, during her time, it touched the highest point of influence and circulation, as the organ of no clique, but the consistent advocate of high principles, and just, consistent, sound (not mere "Liberal Party") political action. As to the subjects of the *Daily News* articles, they ranged over the whole field of public interests, excepting only those " hot and hot " topics which had to be treated immediately that fresh news about them reached London. Those who were with Mrs. Martineau tell me that the only difficulty with her was to choose what subject she would treat each day, out of the many that offered. She kept up an extensive correspondence, and read continually; and her fertile mind, highly cultivated as it was by her life-long studies, had some original and valuable contribution to make upon a vast variety of the topics of which each day brought suggestions.

The marvel that a sick lady, shut up in her house in a remote village, could thus keep touch with, and take an active part in, all the interests and movements of the great world, increases the more it is considered. The very correspondence by which she was aided in knowing and feeling what the public mind was stirred about, was in itself a heavy labour, and a great tax upon such feeble strength as she possessed. The letters with which Mr. Reeve has favoured me give glimpses of how ideas and calls came to her sometimes. Here is a graphic account, for instance, of a man riding up with a telegram from Miss Nightingale—" Agitate! agitate! for Lord de Grey in place of Sir G. Cornewall Lewis,"—which gives the first intimation in Ambleside that the post of War Minister is vacant. The newspaper arrives later, and Lewis's death is learned; so a "leader" is written early next morning, to catch the coach, and appears in the following morning's *Daily News*. Presently Lord de Grey is appointed, and then the two women friends rejoice together in the chance of getting army reforms made by a Minister who, they hope, will not be a slave to royal influences. Another time she tells Mr. Reeve how she is treating the *Reversion of Mysore* in the *Daily News*, on the suggestion of a man learned in

Indian affairs; and again, that she is reviewing a book
of Eastern travel at the request of a friend.  In fine,
there were constant letters seeking to engage her interest and aid in every description of reforms, and for
all kinds of movements in public affairs.

But with all the wide circle of suggesting correspondents, the wonder of the prolific mind working so
actively from the Ambleside hermitage remains untouched.  Perhaps I cannot better show how much
she did, and how wide a range she covered, in *Daily
News* "leaders," than by giving a list of the articles of
a single year.  I take 1861, really at random.  It was
simply the page at which the office ledger happened to
be opened before me.

Here are the subjects of her *Daily News* "leaders"
in 1861 :

The American Union—The King of Prussia—Arterial Drainage
—Sidney Herbert—The Secession of South Carolina—Cotton Sup-
ply—Labourers' Dwellings—The American Difficulty (two days)—
Destitution and its Remedy—The American Revolution—Cotton
Culture—The American Union—Indian Affairs—America : North
and South—American Politics—Agricultural Labour—The London
Bakers—President Buchanan—The Southern Confederacy—United
States Population—The Duchess of Kent—Indian Famines—Agri-
cultural Statistics—President Lincoln's Address—Indian Currency
—American Census—The Southern Confederacy—The Action of
the South—The Census—America and Cotton — The American
Envoy—Lord Canning's Address—The American Crisis—Spain and
San Domingo—East Indian Irrigation—Water-mills—Hayti and
San Domingo—The Conflict in America—American Movements—
The Secession Party—The American Contest—The Literary Fund
—Working-men's Visit to Paris—Mr. Clay's Letter—The American
Contest—Money's "Java" (four articles) — Mr. Douglas — Our
American Relations—Lord Campbell—Results of American Strife
—Our Cotton Supply—American Union—Soldiers' Homes—Indian
Irrigation — San Domingo — American Movements — Slavery in
America—The Morrill Tariff—Drainage in Agriculture—Neutrality
with America—The Builders' Strike—Lord Herbert—Lord Elgin's

Government—The Builders' Dispute—The Strike—The American
Contest—Indian Famines—Syrian Improvement—Affairs of Hayti
—Cotton Supply—The American War and Slavery—Mr. Cameron
and General Butler—Post-office Robberies—The American Press—
Mrs. Stowe — The Morrill Tariff — American Affairs — Domestic
Servants—The Education Minutes—The Georgian Circular—French
Free Trade—The Fremont Resolution—Labourers' Improvidence—
American Humiliation—The Education Code—A Real Social Evil—
Captain Jervis in America—The American Contest—Indian Cotton
—Slaves in America—The Prince of Wales—American Movements
—Lancashire Cotton Trade—India and Cotton—Cotton-growing—
The Herbert Testimonial—Captain Wilkes' Antecedents—Arterial
Drainage—The American Controversy—Land in India—Slaves in
America—Death of Prince Albert—Slavery—Loyalty in Canada—
Review of the Year, five columns long.

This gives a total of one hundred and nine leading
articles, in that one year, on political and social affairs.
In the same year, she wrote to the Boston *Anti-Slavery
Standard* as much matter as would have made about
forty-five " leaders "; and during the same period she
regularly contributed to *Once a Week** a fortnightly
article on some current topic, and also a series of
biographical sketches entitled " Representative Men."
These *Once a Week* articles were all much longer than
"leaders "; the year's aggregate of space filled, in
1861, is two hundred and eighty-one of the closely-
printed columns of *Once a Week*; and this would be
equivalent to at least one hundred and forty leading
articles in the usual " leaded " type. I need not give
a complete list of titles of the year's *Once a Week*
articles; but a few may be cited to show what class
of subjects she selected : "Our Peasantry in Progress,"
"Ireland and her Queen," " The Harvest," "The
Domestic Service Question," "What Women are Educated for," "American Soldiering," "Deaths by Fire,"

* Most of these papers are signed " From the Mountain."

"The Sheffield Outrages," " Education and the Racing Season."

Such was Harriet Martineau's work for the year 1861; and thus could she, confined to her house, comprehend and care for the condition of mankind.

It will be noticed that she had written on Domestic Servants both in the *Daily News* and *Once a Week*; but still she had not said all that she wished to say about the subject, and early in the next year she wrote a long article on it, which appeared in the *Edinburgh* for April, 1862. It is a capital article, distinguished alike by common-sense, and by wide-reaching sympathy; *womanly* in the best sense—in its domestic knowledge, and its feeling for women in their perplexities and troubles, whether as servants or mistresses, —and yet philosophical in its calmness, its power of tracing from causes to effects, and its practical wisdom in forestalling future difficulties.

In this year she began to write historical stories, " Historiettes " as she called them, for *Once a Week*. As fictions, they are not equal to her best productions of that class; but their special value was less in this direction, or even in the detailed historical knowledge that they displayed, than in the insight into the philosophy of political history which the reader gained. They were illustrated by Millais, and proved so attractive that they were continued during the next two years. One, dealing with the constitutional struggle in the reign of Charles I., and called " The Hampdens," has been republished so recently as 1880.

A large portion of her time and thought was absorbed, in these years, by the American struggle and its consequences. Loving the United States and their people as she did, the interest and anxiety with which she watched their progress were extreme. She was no coward—as it is, no doubt, hardly necessary to remark on this page—and though she grieved deeply for the sufferings both of personal friends and of the whole country, yet her soul rose up in noble exultation over the courage, the resolution, and the high-mindedness of the bulk of the American nation. Over here, she threw herself with warm eagerness into the effort to support those Lancashire workers upon whom fell so heavy a tax of deprivation in the Cotton famine. The patience, the quietness, the heroism with which our North-Country workers bore all that they had to suffer, supported as they were by the sympathy of the mass of their fellow-countrymen, and by their own intelligent convictions that they were aiding a good cause by remaining peaceful and quiet—this was just the sort of thing to arouse all Harriet Martineau's loving sympathies. " Her face would all light up and the tears would rush to her eyes whenever she was told of a noble deed," says Miss Arnold ; "no matter how humble the doer, or how small the matter might seem, you could see the delight it gave her to know that a fine, brave, or unselfish act had been done." Animated by such respectful joy in the attitude of the Lancashire workers, she threw herself into their service ; and her correspondence on this topic during 1861, when she used all her public and private influence on their behalf, and employed her best energies in aiding and advising the relief committees, would fill a large volume.

In the midst of her labours for America, she could not but be gratified by the testimonies which constantly reached her from that country to the appreciation of the work which she had done and was doing. *The History of the Peace* was reprinted in Boston in the very midst of the Civil War, "at the instance of men of business throughout the country, who believe it will do great good from its political and yet more economical lessons, which are so much wanted." The publishers of the *Atlantic Monthly* appealed to her to write them a series of articles on "Military Hygiene"; and, over-pressed as she was, she could not refuse a request which enabled her to do much good service for the soldiers of the North, for whom she felt so deeply. Nor were more private tributes to the value of her efforts lacking. A set of the *Rebellion Record*, published by Putnam, was sent to her with the cover stamped under the title with these words—"Presented by Citizens of New York to Harriet Martineau"; and innumerable books came with testimonies inscribed by the writers, such as that in Henry Wilson's *Slave Power in America*, which was as follows:—"Mrs. Harriet Martineau; with the gratitude of the Author for her friendship for his country, and her devotion to freedom."*

---

* The highest honour yet done to her memory is the work of our sisters and brothers across the Atlantic. A public subscription has raised funds for a statue of Harriet Martineau, which has been executed by Anne Whitney, in white marble. The statue represents Mrs. Martineau seated, with her hands folded over a manuscript on her knees. The head is raised, and has a light veil thrown over the back of it and falling down upon the shoulders, while a shawl is draped partially over the figure. The eyes are looking forth, as though in that thoughtful questioning of the future to which she often gave herself. The statue was unveiled in the Old South Hall, Boston, on December 26th, 1883, in the presence of many notable personages. Mrs. Mary Livermore presided, and speeches were made by William Lloyd Garrison, jun., and Wendell Phillips. In the case of the last-named it was his final speech, for he, too, six weeks after, was numbered amongst those who are at rest. "The audience sat in silence for a moment as the white vision was unveiled; then went up such applause as stirred the echoes of the historic interior in which the ceremony took place."

In the latter part of the year 1862, Harriet Martineau wrote a paper on " Our Convict System," which appeared in the following January number of the *Edinburgh*. It will be noted that she never wrote on the politics of the day—the action of the Government and Opposition of the moment—in this *Review*; her political principles were too democratic for the great Whig organ.

In *Once a Week*, however, her articles became more decisively political year by year. Some of her best political papers are in that magazine for 1863. The most noteworthy features in them are their basis of principles and not of party, and their practical wisdom. When I speak of her devotion to principles, in politics, I half fear that I may be misunderstood—for so shockingly does Cant spawn its loathsomeness over every holy phrase, that such expressions come to us " defamed by every charlatan," and doubtful in their use. But she was neither doctrinaire, nor blind, nor pig-headed, nor pharisaic, nor jealous, nor scheming ; but wise, brave, truthful, upright, and independent. Love of justice and truthfulness of speech were as much to her in public affairs as they are to any high-minded person in private. Her desire in her thoughts and utterances on politics was simply to secure " the greatest happiness for the greatest number" of the people ; and the spirit in which she worked was cor-rectly appraised by the then editor of the *Daily News*, William Weir, when he wrote to her in these terms, in 1856 :—

I have never before met—I do not hope again to meet—one so earnest [as you] to promote progress, so practical in the means by which to arrive at it. My aim in life is to be able to say, when it is closing, "I, too, have done somewhat, though little, to benefit my kind"; and there are so few who do not regard this as Quixotism or hypocrisy, that I shrink even from confessing it.

He so well recognised that as truly *her* aim also, that
he did not fear to utter to her his high aspiration. It is
in this spirit that her political articles are written; and
the result of the constant reference to principles is that
her essays are almost as instructive reading now as they
were when first published; *then,* their interest and
their importance were both incalculable.

Of such articles Harriet Martineau wrote in the
*Daily News,* from first to last, *sixteen hundred and
forty-two* : besides the great number that I have
referred to, which appeared in other journals. I
wonder how many of the men who have presumed
to say that women are "incapable of understanding
politics," or of "sympathising in great causes," received a large part of their political education, and of
rousing stimulus to public-spirited action, from those
journalistic writings by Harriet Martineau?

An instructive article on "The Progress of the Negro
Race" was prepared for the *Edinburgh* of January,
1864. Only a few weeks after the appearance of this,
there fell upon her the greatest blow of her old age.
Her beloved niece Maria, who had for so long filled
the place of a daughter to her, was taken ill with
typhoid fever, and died after a three weeks' illness.
Maria Martineau's active disposition, and her intellectual power (which was far above the average), had
made her an ideal companion for her aunt, and the
blow to *her* was a terrible one. Ill and suffering as
she was before, this shock completed the wreck of
Harriet Martineau's health. She had a dreary time of
illness immediately after her niece's death; and although
she went on writing for some time longer, it was
always with the feeling that the end of her long life's
industry was near at hand.

She was not left alone; for Maria's youngest
sister, Jane, presently offered voluntarily to fill, as
far as she could, the vacant place at "The Knoll."
The family from which these sisters came was one
in which kindliness and generosity were (and are
to this day, with its younger members who remain)
distinguishing features. It was no light matter for
Mr. and Mrs. Robert Martineau to part with a
second daughter to their sister; but, as it was Jane's
own wish to try to be to that beloved and honoured
relative what Maria had been, the parents would not
refuse their permission. Harriet wrote of this to Mr.
Reeve with her heart full; telling him how "humbly
grateful" she felt for what was so generously offered
to her, and with what thankfulness she accepted the
blessing. Even in such circumstances, she could
note what a delight it was to find that Maria's own
spirit of devotedness prevailed amongst them all—for
nothing could be nobler and sweeter than the conduct
of everyone.

By June of that same year, 1864, Mrs. Martineau
was ready to undertake another article on a topic
which pressed upon her mind, "Co-operative Societies,"
which was published in the *Edinburgh* for October
following.

She went on writing for the *Daily News,* through
that year and the next, though the effort came to be
constantly more and more laborious. Her interest
in public affairs did not flag; nor is there the least sign
of failure of power in her letters; but she became
increasingly conscious that it was a strain upon her to
write under the responsibility of addressing the public.

Early in 1865 she wrote some articles on "The
Scarcity of Nurses," "poked up to do it," as she said,

by Florence Nightingale. In the April of the same year was prepared an article on " Female Convicts," which was published in the *Edinburgh* for October. In sending this she intimated to the Editor that it would be her last contribution, as she felt the strain of such writing too great for her strength. After all she did prepare one more article for the *Edinburgh,* though it was as long afterwards ás 1868. This was the paper on " Salem Witchcraft," which will be found in the number of that *Review* for July. It formed Harriet Martineau's last contribution of any length to literature ; and she wrote it with some reluctance, after having suggested the subject to Mr. Reeve, and he having replied that he could find no one suitable to undertake it but herself.

She was very loath to cease her writing for the *Daily News,* and continued it until the spring of 1866. It was a great trial when at last the moment came that she felt she absolutely *must* be freed from the obligation and the temptation to frequent work. But the spring was always her worst time as to health ; and during this customary vernal exacerbation of illness, in April 1866, she found herself obliged at last, after fourteen years' service, to send in her resignation to the *Daily News.*

When she thus terminated her connection with the paper through whose columns she had spoken so long, she practically concluded her literary life. Neither her intellectual powers, nor her interest in public affairs, were perceptibly diminished ; as will presently be seen, these continued to the end of her life all but unabated. Her regular literary exertions were now, however, at an end ; and she was ill enough by this time, her niece tells me, to feel only relief at being freed from the constant pressure of the duty of thought and speech.

# CHAPTER XI.

## THE LAST YEARS.

HARRIET MARTINEAU had never gone the right way to work to become rich by literature. She had not chosen her subjects with a view to the mere monetary success she might attain, and, not infrequently, she had displayed a rare generosity in her pecuniary affairs. In April 1867, she was plunged into perplexity about the means of living, by the temporary failure of the Brighton Railway to pay its dividends. After all her work, she had but little to lose. She had from investments in the Preference Stock of that railway £230 per annum, and she had only £150 yearly from all other sources. Such was the fortune saved, after labours such as hers, through a long life of industry and thrift. There was a beautiful contest between the inmates of that home, when the trouble came, as to which of them should begin to make the necessary sacrifices involved in economising. Miss Jane Martineau and the maid Caroline were each ready with their offers, and the invalid mistress of the house was with difficulty induced to continue her wine and dinner ale, while she declared, with a brave assumption of carelessness, that she should be rather glad than otherwise to be rid of seeing the *Times* daily and getting the periodic box of books from "Mudie's." It is touching to note how she tried to lightly pass off this sacrifice of current literature, when one knows that reading was the chief solace of her lonely and suffering days. Her family intervened, however, to prevent any such deprivations, and by-and-by the Company resumed payment of its dividends.

In 1868, she received a generous offer, which touched her very deeply. Mr. J. R. Robinson, of the *Daily News*, proposed to her that there should be a reprint of the several biographical sketches which she had contributed to the paper during her connection with it; and he offered to take all the trouble and responsibility of putting the volume through the press, while leaving to her the whole of the profits. She had not even supposed that the copyright in the biographies which she had written for the paper from time to time, upon the occasions of the deaths of eminent persons, remained her property. Mr. Robinson had the satisfaction of assuring her that the proprietors held her at liberty to reproduce these writings, and, with that comrade's generosity which is not altogether rare among journalists, her kind friend devoted himself to securing her a good publisher, and editing the volume, *Biographical Sketches*, for her benefit. These vignettes well deserved reproduction. She had had more or less personal acquaintance with nearly every one of the forty-six eminent persons of whom she treated; and the portraits which she sketched were equally vivid and impartial. The work was received by the public with an enthusiasm which repaid Mr. Robinson for his generous efforts. It was reprinted in America; and it is now in its fourth English edition.

The last occasion upon which she was to give her powers and her influence to a difficult but great public work must now be mentioned. It was the final effort of her career. Marked as that life had been all through by devotedness to public duty, she never before was engaged in a task so painful and difficult, or one which, upon mere personal grounds, she might more strongly have desired to evade. But at near seventy years old, and so enfeebled that she had thought her work quite finished, she no more hesitated to come to the front under fire when it became necessary, than she had done in those active younger days when combat may have had its own delights.

The subject was an Act of Parliament passed in 1869, having reference to certain police powers over women in various large towns. "In our time, or in any other," wrote Mrs. Martineau, "there never was a graver question." It was clear to her that if women "did not insist upon the restoration of the most sacred liberties of half the people of England, men alone would never do it"; and she wrote four letters on the subject to the *Daily News*, as powerful, as sensible, as free from cant of any kind, as clear in the appreciation of facts, and as definite and able in the presentation of them, as anything she had ever written. She wrote, also, and signed an "Appeal to the Women of England" upon the subject, where her name headed the list of signers, whilst that of Florence Nightingale came next. Two such women, venerated not less for the intellectual capacity and practical wisdom than for the devoted benevolence that they had shown in their long lives, were well able to arouse and lead the moral sense of the womanhood of England in this crisis. Other respected names were soon added to theirs; but it would not be easy to over-estimate the value of the self-sacrificing, brave action, at the most critical moment, of these two great and honourable women.

Besides writing articles and appeals, and signing documents which were placarded as election posters in some great towns, Mrs. Martineau helped that cause in the way told in the following letter to Mr. Atkinson.

May 21st, 1871.

One pleasant thing has happened lately. I *longed* for money for a public object [Repeal of the Acts in question], and, unable to do better, worked a chair, and had it beautifully made up. It was produced at a great evening party in London, and seized upon and vehemently competed for, and it has actually brought—fifty guineas! In the middle of the night it occurs to me what a thing it is to give fifty guineas—so much as I had longed for money to give that fund. I was asked for a letter of explanation and statement to go with the chair, and, of course, did it by that post.

Work for this cause formed the most keen and active interest of her latest years. In this she thought and laboured constantly. She gave her name and support to other objects, but only quietly. Amongst other things, she was a member of the Women's Suffrage Society; and she was a subscriber to the movement for the medical education of women.

In all public affairs, indeed, her interest remained keen and unabated to the very last, as the letters for which I am indebted to Mr. Atkinson, and which I am about to quote, will abundantly show. These letters will indicate, too, something of the quiet course of her now uneventful daily life. Sick and weary as she was, it will be seen that literature and politics, the public welfare, and the concerns of her household's inmates, still occupied her thoughts and her pen.

August 24, 1870.

. . . I am as careful as possible to prevent anyone losing sleep on my account, and being disturbed at meals, or failing in air, exercise, and pleasure. If these regular healthy habits of my household become difficult, we are to have a trained nurse at once. This is settled. I am disposed to think, myself, that the last stage will be short, probably the end sudden.

The tone of this last sentence is no affectation. " She used to talk about her death as if it meant no more than going into the next room," said one who knew her in these years.

September 10, 1870.

. . . I am not sure whether you have read Dr. Bence Jones's *Life and Letters of Faraday*. I have been thankful, this last week, for the strong interest of that book, which puts Continental affairs out of my head for hours together. The first half volume is rather tiresome—giving us four times as much as necessary of the uncultivated youth's early prosings on crude moralities, &c. It is quite right to give us *some* of this, to show from how low a point of thought and style he rose up to his perfection of expression as a lecturer and writer; but a quarter of the early stuff would have been enough for that. The succeeding part, for hundreds of pages, is the richest treat I have had for many a day. I can only distantly and dimly follow the scientific lectures and writings; but I understand enough for sympathy; and the disclosure of the moral nature of the man is perfectly exquisite. I have never known, and have scarcely dreamed of, a spirit and temper so thoroughly uniting the best attributes of the sage and the child.

October 18, 1870.

I had my envelope directed yesterday, but was prevented writing, and in the evening came your welcome letter. I am glad to know *when* you mean to leave your quarters; and every line from France is interesting.

I wonder whether you remember a night in London when dear Mrs. Reid and you and I were returning in her carriage from Exeter Hall and the *Messiah*. I was saying that that sacred drama reminded me of Holy Philæ, and the apotheosis of Osiris, and how the one was as true as the other, with its "Peace on earth, and good-will to men," so false a prophecy, &c. &c. Whereupon Mrs. Reid said, plaintively (of the *Messiah*), "I believe it all at the time," but she did not set up any pretence of the promises having been fulfilled. It does not seem as if Christendom had got on very much since the world said, "See how these Christians love one another!" I seem to have got to a new state of mind about war, or I may perhaps forget the emotions of youth; but I seem never before to have felt the horror, disgust, shame—in short, misery— that the spectacle of this war creates now. I am reading less and less in the newspapers; for, the truth is, I cannot endure it. There is no good in any *hopeless* spectacle; and for France, I am, like most people, utterly hopeless. . . . By selling themselves for twenty years to the worst and meanest man in Europe, the people of France have incurred destruction; and though most of us knew this all the time, we do not suffer the less from the spectacle now. . . . I suppose the French will have no alternative but peace in a little while; but, when all that is settled, internal strife and domestic ruin will remain ahead. The truth is, the *morale* of the French is corrupted to the core. All habit of integrity and sincerity is apparently lost; and when a people prefers deception to truth, vainglory to honour, passion to reason—all is over. I will leave it, for it is a terrible subject. I must just say that I believe and know that there *are* French citizens—a very few—who understand the case, but they are as wretched as they necessarily must be. But "the gay licentious proud," the pleasure-loving, self-seeking aristocracy, and the brutally ignorant rural population, must entirely paralyse the intelligent and honest few scattered in their midst. But I must leave all this.

The only news we have is of the royal marriage [Princess Louise] which pleases everybody. It is really a great event—as a sign politically, and as a fact socially and morally. After the Queen's marriage, I wrote repeatedly on behalf of repealing the Royal Marriage Act *then*, while there could be no invidious appearance in it. The present chaotic condition of Protestant princedoms in Germany may answer the purpose almost as well as a period of abeyance. Any way, the relaxation seems a wise and happy one.

My items of news are small in comparison,—but not small to me; especially that a happy idea struck me lately, of trying a spring mattress as a means of obtaining sleep of some continuance. I have ventured upon getting one; and, after four nights, there is no doubt of my being able to sleep longer and with more loss of consciousness than for a very long time. Last night I once slept three hours with only one break. Otherwise, I go on much the same. There is one objection to these beds which healthy people are unaware of—that so much more strength is required to move in bed, from want of *purchase*. This *is* a trouble, but the advantages far outweigh it.

Dear Jenny comes home to-morrow evening, all the better, I am assured, for three weeks at the sea, in breeze and sun, and all manner of beauty of land and sea (at Barmouth, and with a merry party of young people). And here is a game basket, arrived from parts unknown, with a fine hare, two brace of partridges, and a pheasant. A savoury welcome for Jenny! Cousin Mary has been more good and kind than I can say. She stays for Jenny, and leaves us on Friday. I must not begin upon Huxley, Tyndall, and Evans, whom I have been reading. Much pleasure to you, dear friend, in your closing weeks.

Yours ever,

H. MARTINEAU.

The sleepless nights repeatedly mentioned in these letters were a source of great suffering to her in these latest years; under medical advice, she tried smoking as a means of procuring better rest, with some success. She smoked usually through the chiboque which she had brought home with her from the East, and which she had there learned to use, as she relates with her customary simplicity and directness in the appendix to *Eastern Life*: "I found it good for my health," she says there, "and I saw no more reason why I should not take it than why English ladies should not take their glass of sherry at home—an indulgence which I do not need. I continued the use of my chiboque for some weeks after my return, and then only left it off because of the inconvenience." When health and comfort were to be promoted by it, she resumed it. Her nights were, nevertheless, very broken, and frequent allusions occur in her letters to the suffering of sleeplessness, with its concomitant of drowsiness in the day-time.

The next letter is on trivial topics, truly; but is none the less valuable for the unconscious record which it affords of her domestic character. The anxiety for her household companion's enjoyment, the delight in the kindness that the young folk had shown to each other and to the poor Christmas guests, the pleasure in the happiness of other people, are all characteristic features which are of *no trivial* consequence.

Ambleside, Jan. 2, '71.

I am so sorry for the way you are passing from the old year to the new that I cannot help saying so. I ought to be anything but sorry, considering what good you are doing—essential, indispensable good; but you must be so longing for your own quiet, warm home, and the friends around it, that I heartily wish you were there. . . . As for me, my business is to promote, as far as possible, the cheerfulness of my household. There really has been much fun,—and yet more sober enjoyment, throughout this particular Christmas. In my secret mind I am nervously anxious about Jenny, to whom cold is a sort of poison; but, when she had once observed that there was much less cold here than at home, or anywhere else that she could be, I determined to say no more, and to make the best of it. She said it for my sake, I know (the only reason for her ever speaking of herself), and I frankly received it as a comfortable saying. She is getting on better than any of us expected, and she has been thoroughly happy in exercising our hospitalities. . . . Jenny's brother Frank came for three days at Christmas; and Harriet made herself housekeeper and secretary, and made Jenny the guest, to set her wholly at liberty for her brother. It was quite a pretty sight—they were all so happy! There was a kitchen party on Christmas Day; by far the best we ever had; for Frank did the thing thoroughly—read a comic tale, taught the folk games, played off the snapdragons, and finally produced boxes of new and strange crackers, which spat forth the most extraordinary presents! All the guests and the servants were in raptures with him. The oldest widow but one vowed that "she did not know *when* she had seen such a gentleman"—which I think very probable. They came to dinner at noon, and stayed till past 10 p.m. Think of spending those ten hours entirely in the two kitchens, and having four meals in the time! My nieces, *and nephew, were* tired! So was I, though I had only the consciousness of the occasion. . . . All this is so good for Jenny! and she will like the quiet and leisure that will follow. . . .

I am more alive and far less suffering than in the great heats of autumn. Your slips and cuttings are very interesting, and I am very thankful for them. More of them when (or if) my head is worth more. Of course, we shall hear when you get home. May it be soon!

Yours ever, dear friend,

H. MARTINEAU.

Ambleside, March 6, '71.

*We* are in a queer state just now. Gladstone turns out *exactly* as I expected. I once told some, who are his colleagues now, that he would do some very fine deeds—give us some separate measures of very great value, and would do it in an admirable manner; but that he would show himself incapable of governing the country. For two years he did the first thing; and now, this third year, he is showing the expected incapacity. Were there ever such means thrown away as we see this session? Probably you are out of the way of hearing the whole truth of the situation, and I cannot go into it here. Suffice it, that Gladstone totters (and three or four more), and that several departments are in such a mess and muddle that one hardly sees how they are to be brought straight again; and all this without the least occasion! One matter, in which I feel deep interest, and on which I have acted, is prospering, and we have the Government at our disposal; so that we hope they will remain in office till we have secured what we want; but the more we have to do with Ministers, the weaker we find them. And Gladstone is not only weak as a reasoner (with all his hair-splitting), but ignorant in matters of political principle.

The next letter is very characteristic and perfectly true to her state of mind with regard to flutterers.

May 21, '71.

And now, you will want to know how Miss —— and we fared this day week. We (she and I) were together only three-quarters of an hour; and for part of that time I was too much exhausted to benefit much. My impression is that she is not ex-actly the person for the invalid room. But I may be utterly wrong in this. I might be misled by the fatiguing sort of annoyance of overpraise—of worship in fact. I don't want to be ungracious about what my books were to her in her childhood and youth; I am quite ready to believe her sincere in what she said. But not the less is it bad taste. It must be bad taste to expatiate on that one topic which it is most certain that the hearer cannot sympathise in. Also, I have much doubt of her being accurate in her talk. There is a random air about her statements, and she said two or three things that certainly were mistakes, more or less. These things, and a general smoothness. in her talk, while she was harsh about some of the —— were what I did not quite like. As for the rest, she was as kind as possible; and not only kind to me, but evidently with a turn that way, and a habit of it in regard to children, and friends. . .

June 11, '71.

. . . Of all odd tnings, Dean Stanley and Lady Augusta have been, by way of a trip, to Paris, from last Monday to Saturday. How *can* they! One would think nothing could take one there but some strong call of duty. The least that one must read and hear is enough to make one's heart ache, and to spoil one's sleep, and to disfigure life till one does not wish to look at it any more. I do long to have done with it. I believe it is the first occasion in my life of my having felt hopeless of any destiny, individual or national. . . . How badly our public affairs are going! Gladstone and Co. are turning out exactly as many of us foresaw. The thing nearest my heart [Repeal of the Acts above alluded to], and more important than all other public questions, will do well. It is, I believe, secure, in virtue of an amount of effort and devotedness never surpassed. You know what I mean. I rest upon that achievement—a vital aim with me and others for many years— with satisfaction and entire hopefulness, but in all other directions the prospect is simply dreary. In that one case, we, who shall have achieved the object, have saved Ministers from themselves, and from evil councillors. Wherever they have, this year, trusted their own wisdom and resources, they have failed, or see that they must fail. They would have been *out* since early in April, but for want of a leader on the Conservative side; and they still make their party dwindle till there will be no heart or energy left in the Liberal ranks—lately so strong and ardent! They may be individually clever; but they cannot govern the country. This is eminently the case with Gladstone; and it may serve as the description of the group. I shall not dare to ask the Arnolds about such matters—so thoroughly did they assume, when they went away, that all must be right with "William" and Co. in the Cabinet.

Nov. 5, '71.

. . . Mrs. Grote seems to like to open her feelings to me, as a very old friend of hers and her husband's. Did I tell you that she sent me—to put me in possession of her state—her private Diary, from the first day of her alarm about her husband's health to the day she sent it ? It was more interesting than I can say; but it brought after it something more striking still. Some half-century ago, Jeremy Bentham threw upon paper some thoughts on the operation of Natural Religion on human welfare, or *ill*-fare. His MSS. were left to Mrs. Grote (or portions of them), and those papers were issued by the Grotes under the title, *Analysis of the Influence of Natural Religion*, &c. &c., by " Philip Beauchamp." It is a tract of 142 pp. It is the boldest conceivable effort at fair play; and, in this particular effect, it is most striking. At the outset, all attempts to divide the " abuses " of religion from other modes of operation are repudiated at once; and the claim is so evidently sound that the effect of the exposure is singular. Well ! of course the tendency of the exposition is to show that the absolute darkness of the Unseen Life supposed must produce a demoralising effect, and destroy ease of mind. There is something almost appalling in the unflinching representation of the mischief of the spirit of fear, of its torment, and of its damaging effects in creating a habit of adulation, in perverting the direction of our desires, in corrupting our estimate of good and evil, in leaving us, in short, no chance of living a healthy and natural life, but rather, making cowards, liars, and selfish rascals of us all. I can't go on, being tired ; and you will be thinking, as you read, that this is only the old story—of the mischiefs and miseries of superstition. But there is something impressive in the cheerful simplicity with which Bentham tells us his opinion of the sort of person recommended to us for a Master under the name of God, and with which he warns us all of the impossibility of our being good or happy under such a Supreme Being. In looking at the table of contents, and seeing the catalogue he gives of the evil effects of belief in the barest scheme of Natural Religion' one becomes aware, as if for the first time, of the atmosphere of falsehood against which we ought to have recoiled all our lives, since becoming capable of thought.

Dec. 30, '71.

. . . I go off rapidly as a correspondent; there is no use blinking the fact. I am so slow, and write so badly ! and leave off *too* tired. Oddly enough, this very week one of the *Daily News* authorities has been uttering a groaning longing for my pen in the service of that paper, as of old. The occasion is a short letter of

mine in last Thursday's paper, which you may have seen.* If so,
you will see that I had no choice. W. E. Forster was at Fox How;
and I got Jenny to carry the volume of Brougham (vol. iii. p. 302)
to consult Forster and Arnolds about what I should do, W. E.
Forster being in the same line of business with my father, and a
public man—man of the world. He was clear: it was impossible
to leave my father under a false imputation of having failed. And
when my letter appeared, he was delighted with it; so are those
of my family that I have heard from; and, above all, *Daily News*
Editors. They hope and believe it will excite due distrust of
Brougham's representations, and encourage others to expose his
falsehoods. His suppressions are as wonderful as his disclosures;
*e.g.* the very important crisis in his career, known by the name of
the "Grey Banquet" at Edinburgh, he cuts completely out of the
history of the time—perverting Lord Durham's story as well as his
own. I can see how the false story of me and mine got made;
but enough of that—especially if you have *not* seen the letter in
the *Daily News*. Forster was kindly and quiet, but he *is* altered.
He is now—the Courtier!—an odd sort of one, with much Quaker
innocence and prudence in it; but of a sort which leaves me no
hope of *his* handling of his Education measure. There will be
such a fight! and the Nonconformists are right, and know that
they are. You will probably see *that* achieved—a real National
Education established, secular and compulsory.

The Ambleside surgeon, who had undertaken, in
accordance with Harriet Martineau's will, to prepare
and transmit her skull and brain to Mr. Atkinson,
died in the year 1872. The following letter shows
that the progress of time had in no way diminished
her willingness to leave her head for scientific investigation.

Ambleside, April 23, '72.

(Shakespere's birthday and Wordsworth's deathday.)

DEAR FRIEND,

I am not writing about poets to-day, nor about an
"play" topic, nor anything gay, or pretty, or amusing. I write
on business only.

---

* Refuting a statement made in Lord Brougham's *Autobio
graphy* that her father had failed in business.

When you heard of Mr. Shepherd's death, you must, I should think, have considered what was to be done in regard to fulfilling the provision of my will about skull and brain. It is to inform you of this that I write.

Mr. Shepherd's assistant and successor is *Mr. William Moore King*, a young man who is considered very clever, and is certainly very kind, gentlemanly, simple in mind and manners, and married to a charming girl (grand-daughter of Martin, the artist). Jenny has known them for two years, having called on their arrival. I had seen him twice before this last week. I wrote to him the other day, to ask him to give me half an hour for confidential conversation; and he came when I was quite alone for the morning.

I told him the whole matter of the provision in my will, and of Mr. Shepherd's engagement, in case of his surviving me in sufficient vigour to keep his word. Mr. King listened anxiously, made himself master of the arrangement, and distinctly engaged to do what we ask, saying that it was so completely clear between us that we need never speak of it again.

I may add that Mr. King has shown me the letters in which Mrs. Martineau made the necessary arrangements with him for his task. Mr. Atkinson was, however, now residing out of England, and not in a position to usefully accept the bequest, so he intimated his desire to be freed from his promise to undertake the examination of his friend's brain. A codicil was added to Harriet Martineau's will, therefore, revoking the provision about this matter.

The next quotation shows how little the long prospect of death had changed her expectations and desires about things supernatural :—

November 19, '72.

I mean to try to do justice to what I think and believe, by avowing the satisfaction I truly feel with my release from selfish superstition and trumpery self-regards, and with the calm conclusions of my reason about what to desire and expect in the position in which each one of us mysterious human beings finds him or herself. It is all we have to do now (such as you and I), to be satisfied with the conditions of the life we have left behind us, and fearless of the death which lies before us. Nobody will ever find me craving the "glory and bliss" which the preachers set before us, and pray that we may obtain. Some of them are very good and kind, I know; but they will never create any longing of the sort in me. But why should I scribble on in this way to you? Perhaps because our new Evangelical curate has written me almost the worst and silliest letter of this sort that I ever saw. Enough of him then! But I have left myself no room or strength for other matters this time. I wanted to tell you about the effect—according to my experience—of a second reading of *Adam Bede*, Miss Evans's first great novel. A singular mind is hers, I should think, and truly wonderful in power and scope. Her intellectual power and grace attract and win people of very high intellectual quality.

Miss Jane Martineau was at this time in very delicate health, and, after long fluctuations of hope and fear, was compelled to leave her aunt for the winter and go to a warmer climate. Mrs. Martineau's letters show how cruel was her anxiety for "my precious Jenny," and are filled with expressions of her feelings about the state of her beloved young companion. All this is, of course, too personal for quotation, but a perusal of it amply confirms the accounts of her domestic affection, and the warmth and sensitiveness of her heart.

The loss of her niece from her side ultimately compelled the engagement of a companion, Miss Goodwin, a young lady who became as much attached to Harriet Martineau as did all others who came in close relationship with her in those years.

May 10, '73.

. . . The great event to me and my household is, that Caroline—my dear maid and nurse—has seen Jenny . . . It was such a pouring out on both sides. It would have almost broken Jenny's heart not to have seen this very dear friend of ours, when only half-an-hour off. All her longing is to be by my side again. I never discourage this; but I don't believe it can come to pass. . . . Everbody is kind and helpful; and our admiration of Miss Goodwin ever increases.

DEAR FRIEND,                 Ambleside, Sept. 7th, '73.

I am not ungrateful nor insensible about your treating me with letters, whether I reply or not. You may be sure I *would* write if I could. But you know I cannot, and why. At times I really indulge in the hope and belief that the end is drawing near, and then again, if I compare the present day with a year ago, it seems as if there was no very great change. I still do not make mistakes—or only in trifling slips of memory common enough at seventy. Still I have no haunting ideas, no delusions, no fears,— except that vague sort of misgiving that occurs when it becomes a fatigue to talk, and to move about, and to plan the duties of the day. Yet aware as I am of the character of the change in me, and confident as I still am of not making a fool of myself till I alter further, I now seldom or never (almost never) feel *quite* myself. I have told you this often lately; but I feel as if it would not be quite honest to omit saying it while feeling it to be the most prominent experience of my life at this time. It is not always easy to draw the line as to what one should tell in such a case. On the one hand, I desire to avoid all appearance of weak and tire- some complaining of what cannot be helped; and on the other, I do wish not to appear unaware of my failures. I am sure you understand this, and can sympathise in the anxiety about keeping the balance honest. There have been heart-attacks now and then lately, which have caused digitalis and belladonna to be prescribed for me; and this creates a hope that the general bodily condition is declining in good proportion to the brain weakening. . . . Miss ———— and her naval partner remind me of the pair in the novel that I have read eleven times—Miss Austen's *Persuasion*—un- equalled in interest, charm, and truth (to *my* mind). There is a hint there of the drawback of separation; but yet,—who would have desired anything for Anne Elliot and her Captain Went- worth but that they should marry? I am now in the middle of Miss Thackeray's *Old Kensington*—reading it with much keen pleasure, and some satisfaction and surprise. There are exquisite touches in it; and there is a further disclosure of power, of genuine, substantial, vital power: but her mannerism grows on her deplorably, it seems to me. The amount and the mode of analysis of minds and characters are too far disproportioned to the other elements to be accepted without regret, and, perhaps, some fear for the future. But I have not read half the book yet; and I hope I may have to recall all fault-finding, and to dwell only on the singular value and beauty of the picture-gallery she has given us.

An incident of this year's (1873) story, which must not be overlooked, was an offer of a pension made to Harriet Martineau by Mr. Gladstone. She had written sadly of her own sufferings in a letter to Mrs. Grote, which referred also to Mr. Grote's life, and that lady had published the letter. Mr. Gladstone, in delicate and friendly terms, intimated to Mrs. Martineau that if pecuniary anxiety in any way added to her troubles, he would recommend the Queen to give her one of the literary pensions of the Civil List. She declined it with real gratitude, partly upon the same grounds which had before led her to refuse a similar offer, but with the additional reason now that she would not expose the Queen and the Premier to insult for showing friendliness to " an infidel."

The next letter is mainly domestic, but I am sure that those spoken of by name in it will not object to publication of references in order to show Harriet Martineau n her amiable, considerate household character :—

DEAR FRIEND,                                    December 6, 1873.

I will not trouble and pain you by a long story about the cares and anxieties which make the last stage of my long life hard to manage and to bear. If I could be quite sure of the end being as near as one would suppose, I could bear my own share quietly enough; but it is a different thing watching a younger life going out prematurely. My beloved Jenny will die, after all, we think, bravely as she has borne up for two years. The terrible East winds again got hold of her before she went (so early as October !) to her winter quarters; and there are sudden and grave symptoms of dropsy. The old dread of the post has returned upon me; and I am amazed to find how I can still suffer from fear. I am quite unfit to live alone—even for a week; yet I mean to venture it, if necessary. Miss Goodwin *shall* go (to Leeds) for Christmas Day, on which the family have always hitherto assembled. I will not prevent their doing so now. My niece Harriet (Higginson) was to come, as usual, for a month's holiday at Christmas; but her mother has lamed herself by a fall, and it must be doubtful whether she can be left. Parents protest the dear girl shall come; but she and I wait to see. There is nobody else; for there is illness in all families, or anxiety about illness elsewhere. " Well! we shall be on the other side of it somehow," as people say, and it won't matter much then. My young cook is wanted on Christmas Day to be a bridesmaid, at Nottingham. So I have a real reason for giving up the great Christmas party I have given (in the kitchen) every year till now. It will be costly, giving the people handsome dinners in their own homes; but the house will be quiet, and to me the day will be like any other day. It is not now a time for much mirth: the Arnolds meeting at their mother's grave, my Jenny absent, from perilous illness, my brain failing, so that I can do nothing for anybody but by money (and not very much in that way). We are all disposed to keep quiet—wishing the outside world a " Merry Christmas."

April 15th, 1874.

I am reading again that marvellous *Middlemarch*, finding I did not half value it before. It is not a book to issue as a serial. Yet, read *en suite*, I find it almost more (greater) than I can bear. The Casaubons set me dreaming all night. Do you ever hear *any*thing of Lewes and Miss Evans ?

During the whole of the time over which these letters extend Mrs. Martineau was subject to fainting fits, in any one of which her life might have ended. It was thus necessary for her to have her maid sleeping in her bed-room. Caroline, the " dear friend and servant " for twenty-one years, died early in 1875. Her place was filled by the younger maid, Mary Ann, whom Caroline had trained. The maid has told me of her mistress's kindness and readiness to be amused, of the gentleness of her manner, and the gratitude which she seemed to feel for all loving tendance. The next letter gives a glimpse of the daily life from the mistress's pen :—

Dec. 8, '75.

East winds have been abundantly bitter; but this house is sheltered from the east and north. We do pity the babes and their mothers in the cottages below; and there is no denying that

I am painfully stupified by such cold as we have; but my *aides* and my maids are as well and as happy as if we had the making of the season. It is a daily surprise to me to see how Jenny holds *out* and *on*, without any sort of relapse; yet I *cannot* rise above the anxiety which haunts me in the midst of every night and early morning— dread of hearing that she and Miss Goodwin are ill with the cold which makes *me* so ill. By 6 o'clock I can stay in bed no longer. My maid and I (in the same room) turn out of our beds as the clock strikes; she puts a match to the fire, and goes for my special cup of tea (needed after my bad nights), while I brush my hair. I take the tea to the window, and look out for the lights (Fox How usually the first) as they kindle and twinkle throughout the valley—Orion going down behind Loughrigg as day is breaking. Then I get on the bed for half an hour's reading, till the hot water comes up. By that time I am in a panic about my *aides*; but as soon as I am seated at my little table ready for breakfast, in come the dear creatures, as gay as larks, with news how the glass stands, out-door and in. Out-door (not on the ground) it is somewhere between 32° and 40° at present; and in my room (before the fire has got up), from 50° to 57°. So now you know what our present life and climate are like.

After dinner.—I must end almost before I have begun! But, have you seen, in any newspaper, the address presented to Carlyle on his 80th birthday? I had no doubt about subscribing, and my name is there. I feel great deference for Masson, who asked me; and though I do not agree with all the ascriptions of the Address, there is enough in which I do heartily agree to enable me to sign; so I send my sovereign with satisfaction. I shall not see the medal, not even a bronze one (you know Carlyle's is gold). My expenses are considerable *at present* (not always), and I must not spend on such an object. The way in which the thing was done is delicate. Instead of overwhelming the old man with a deputation, the promoters had the packet quietly left at his door. It would set him weeping for his loneliness,—that his long-suffering, faithful wife did not witness this crowning glory. He does love fame (or *did*), and no man would despise such a tribute as this; but I think he will find it oppressive. What a change since the day when the *Edinburgh Review* was obliged, as Jeffrey said, to decline articles from Carlyle—much as he wished to aid him—because the readers could not tolerate C.'s writings! And that was after his now famous " Burns " article had appeared, and founded his fame in America!

Did you see that the *Times* death-list showed, in two days last week, thirty-three deaths of persons over 70, eleven of whom were over 80 ? The effect of the cold !

. . . The sick and aged will die off fast this winter. May I be one !

DEAR OLD FRIEND, Jan. 25, '76.

It is time that you were hearing from us of the marked increase in my illness within the few days since I last reported of matters of mutual interest. I will not trouble you with disagreeable descriptions of ailments which admit of no advantageous treatment. Last week there was, as twice before (and now again twice), a copious hæmorrhage¹ from some interior part, by which I am much weakened. The cause is not understood; and what does it matter ? I neither know nor much care how it happens that I find myself sinking more rapidly than hitherto. All I know is that I am fully satisfied with my share of the interest and amusement of life, and of the value of the knowledge which has come to me by means of the Brain, which is worth all the rest of us.

I have not much pain, none very severe, but much discomfort. At times I *see* very badly, and *hear* almost nothing; and then I recover more or less of both powers. There is so much cramp in the hands, and elsewhere, that it seems very doubtful whether you and other friends will hear much from me during the (supposed) short time that I shall be living. But I do hope you will let me hear, to the last, of your interests and pursuits, your friendships and companionships, and prospects of increasing wisdom. I cannot write more to-day. Perhaps I may become able another day. My beloved niece Jenny is well; better here than she would be anywhere else, and more happy in her restoration to her home with me than I can describe. I could easily show you how and why my death within a short time may be for the happiness of some whom I love, and who love me; and if it should be the severest trial to this most dear helper of my latter days, I am sure she will bear it wisely and well. It cannot but be the happiest thought in her mind and heart—what a blessing she has been to my old age ! What have not *you* been, dear friend ! I must not enter on that now. Jenny observed this morning that old or delicate people live wonderfully long. True! but I hope my term will be short, if I am to continue as ill as at present.

The end was, indeed, approaching; and now, when at the worst of her illness, it so came about that she was asked and consented to do one last piece of writing for publication. Her young companion, Miss Goodwin, had translated Pauli's *Simon de Montfort*, and Mr. Trübner, unaware, of course, how ill Mrs. Martineau was, offered to publish the translation on the condition that she would write an introduction. She would not refuse this favour to Miss Goodwin, and did the work with great difficulty. It was characteristic that she should think it necessary to take the trouble to *read* the whole MS. before writing her few pages of introduction.

She was now nearing her seventy-fourth birthday; and the strong constitution which had worn through so much pain and labour had almost exhausted its vitality.

Even in these last weeks she could not be idle. Her hands were cramped, her eyes weak, her sensations of fatigue very hard to bear; still, she not only continued her correspondence with one or two of her dearest friends, but also went on with her fancy work. The latter was now of that easiest kind, requiring least effort of eye and thought—knitting. She occupied herself with making cot blankets, in double knitting, for the babies of her young friends; some of them among her poorer neighbours, whom she had known when they were little children themselves and she came first to Ambleside, others among more distant and wealthier couples. She finished one blanket early in the year 1876, for a baby born in Ambleside in the January, and she left a second one unfinished when she died.

Babies were an unfailing delight to her, to the end. Her maids knew that even if she were too ill to see grown-up visitors, a little child was always a welcome guest, for at least a few moments. Her letters to children were altogether charming, and so were her ways with them, and children always loved her with all their wise little hearts. She was a pleasant old lady, even for them to look at. The expression of the countenance became very gentle and motherly, when the strife of working life was laid aside; the eyes were ever kind; and the mouth loved to laugh, sternly and firmly though it could at times be compressed. She wore a large cap of delicate lace, and was dainty about her person, as regarded the fairest cleanliness. Plain in her youth and middle life, she had now grown into a beautiful old age—beauty of the kind which such years can gain from the impress on the features of the high thoughts and elevated emotions of the past, with patience, lovingness, and serenity in the present.

Patient, loving, and serene the last years of Harriet Martineau were. Those who lived with her knew less than her correspondents of what she suffered; for she felt it a duty to tell the absent what they could not see for themselves of her state; but to her household she spoke but seldom, comparatively, of her painful sensations, leaving the matter to their own observation. She could be absorbed to the last in all that concerned the world and mankind; and she was equally accessible to the smaller and more homely interests of the quiet daily life of her inmates. The incidents which go to show what she was in her domestic circle are but trifling; but what is it that makes the difference between an intolerable and a venerable old age (or youth, for the matter of that, in domestic life) except its conduct about trifles? One who was with her tells of her delight when a basket of newly-fledged ducklings was

brought to her bedside, before she was up, on St
Valentine's Day in the year of her death, offering her
a doggrel tribute as follows :—

> St. Valentine hopes you will not scorn
> This little gift on St. Valentine's morn.
> We'd have come with the chime of last ev'ning's bells,
> But, alas! we could not break our shells!

Then another remembers her amusement when one
of her nephews had just started to go to the coach for
London, and the doctor, coming in unannounced, left
his hat on the hall table, which the active servant
seeing, and jumping to the conclusion that Mr. Martineau (travelling in a felt) had left his high hat
behind him, rushed off with it to the coach-office,
half a mile away; so that when the doctor wanted
to go, his hat was off to the coach; and "the old lady
did laugh so." Only a week or two before her death,
she was merry enough to ask her doctor that dreadful
punning conundrum about the resemblance between
an ice-cream vendor and an hydrophobic patient—the
answer turning on the legend "Water ices and ice-
creams" (water I sees, and I screams)—telling him
that it was a *professional* conundrum. At the same
time she was kind enough to repeat to him the com-
pliments which a visitor of hers had been paying his
baby. This was the lighter side of the aged woman's
life, the more serious aspect of which is shown in some
of her letters to Mr. Atkinson. The last of these
letters must now be given :—

DEAR FRIEND,                       Ambleside, May 19, 1876.

Jenny, and also my sister, have been observing that you
ought to be hearing from us, and have offered to write to you.
You will see at once what this means; and it is quite true that
I have become so much worse lately that we ought to guard
against your being surprised, some day soon, by news of my life

being closed. I feel uncertain about how long I *may* live in my present state. I can only follow the judgment of unprejudiced observers; and I see that my household believe the end to be not far off. I will not trouble you with disagreeable details. It is enough to say that I am in no respect better, while all the ailments are on the increase. The imperfect heart-action immediately affects the brain, causing the suffering which is worse than all other evils together,—the horrid sensation of not being quite myself. This strange, dreamy *non-recognition of myself* comes on every evening, and all else is a trifle in comparison. But there is a good deal more. Cramps in the hands prevent writing, and most other employment, except at intervals. Indications of dropsy have lately appeared: and after this, I need not again tell you that I see how fully my household believe that the end is not far off. Meantime I have no cares or troubles beyond the bodily uneasiness (which, however, I don't deny to be an evil). I cannot think of any future as at all probable, except the "annihilation" from which some people recoil with so much horror. I find myself here in the universe,—I know not how, whence, or why. I see everything in the universe go out and disappear, and I see no reason for supposing that it is not an actual and entire death. And for *my* part, I have no objection to such an extinction. I well remember the passion with which W. E. Forster said to me, "I had rather be damned than annihilated." If he once felt five minutes' damnation, he would be thankful for extinction in preference. The truth is, I care little about it any way. Now that the event draws near, and that I see how fully my household expect my death pretty soon, the universe opens so widely before my view, and I see the old notions of death and scenes to follow to be so merely human—so impossible to be true, when one glances through the range of science—that I see nothing to be done but to wait, without fear or hope, or ignorant prejudice, for the expiration of life. I have no wish for further experience, nor have I any fear of it. Under the weariness of illness I long to be asleep; but I have not set my mind on any state. I wonder if all this represents your notions at all. I should think it does, while yet we are fully aware how mere a glimpse we have of the universe and the life it contains.

Above all, I wish to escape from the narrowness of taking a mere human view of things, from the absurdity of making God after man's own image, &c.

But I will leave this, begging your pardon for what may be so unworthy to be dwelt on. However, you *may* like to know how the case looks to a friend under the clear knowledge of death

being so near at hand. My hands are cramped and I must stop.
My sister is here for the whole of May, and she and Jenny are
most happy together. Many affectionate relations and friends are
willing to come if needed (the Browns among others), if I live
beyond July.    You were not among the Boulogne theological
petitioners, I suppose. I don't know whether you can *use* ———
there ? I was very thankful for your last, though I have said
nothing about its contents. If I began *that*, I should not know
how to stop.

So good-bye for to-day, dear friend !

Yours ever,<br>H. M.

The internal tumour which was the prime cause of
her malady (an entirely different kind of thing, however, from that which she suffered from at Tynemouth),
had long been the source of great inconvenience, com-
pelling her to descend the stairs backwards, and to
spend much time in a recumbent position.    The post-
mortem examination made by her medical attendant,
at the request of her executors, two days after she
died, revealed the fact that this tumour was the true
cause of her sufferings.    She never knew it herself.
Relying on the statement of the eminent men whom
she consulted in 1855, that it was the heart that was
affected, she accepted that as her fate.    It was, however, the slow growth of a " dermoid cyst " which
made her linger till such an age, through the constant
suffering of twenty-one preceding years.

In the early part of June 1876 she had an attack of
bronchitis, and though medical treatment subdued this
speedily, it exhausted her strength greatly.    From
about the 14th of that month—two days after her
seventy-fourth birthday—she was confined to her room,
but still rose from bed.    On the 24th she was too ill
to get up.    Then drowsiness gradually increased, and
in a little while she sank quietly into a dreamy state,

in which she seemed to retain consciousness when aroused, but was too weak to either take food or to speak. At last, on the 27th of June, 1876, just as the summer sunset was gilding the hills that she knew and loved so well, she quietly and peacefully drew her last breath, and entered into eternal rest.

Truly her death—not only the last moments, but the long ordeal—might stand for an illustration of the saying of the wise man of old—" Keep innocency, and take heed unto the thing that is right, for *that* shall bring a man peace at the last."

She was buried amidst her kindred, in the old cemetery of Birmingham; and upon the tombstone, where it stands amidst the smoke, there is no inscription beyond her name and age, and the places of birth and death.

More was, perhaps, needless. Her works, and a yet more precious possession, her character, remain. Faults she had, of course—the necessary defects of her virtues. Let it be said that she held her own opinions too confidently—the uncertain cannot be teachers. Let it be said that her personal dislikes were many and strong—it is the necessary antithesis of powerful attachments. Let it be said that her powers of antagonism at times were not sufficiently restrained—how, without such oppugnancy, could she have stood forth for unpopular truths? Let all that detractors can say be said, and how much remains untouched!

In the paths where Harriet Martineau trod at first almost alone, many women are now following. Serious studies, political activity, a share in social reforms, an independent, self-supporting career, and freedom of thought and expression, are, by the conditions of our age, becoming open to the thousands of women who would never have dared to claim them in the circumstances in which she first did so. In a yet earlier age such a life, even to such powers as hers, would have been impossible. As it was, she was only a pioneer of the new order of things inevitable under the advance of civilisation and knowledge. The printing-press, which multiplies the words of the thinker ; the steam-engine, which both feeds the press and rushes off with its product, and the electric telegraph, which carries thought around the globe, make this an age in which mental force assumes an importance which it never had before in the history of mankind. Mind will be more and more valued and cultivated, and will grow more and more influential ; and the condition and status of women must alter accordingly. Some people do not like this fact ; and no one can safely attempt to foresee all its consequences ; but we can no more prevent it than we can return to hornbooks, or to trial by ordeal, or to the feudal tenure of land, or to any other bygone state of social affairs. More and more it will grow customary for women to study such subjects as Harriet Martineau studied ; more commonplace will it constantly become for women to use all their mental faculties, and to exert every one of their powers to the fullest extent in the highest freedom. What, then, have we to wish about that which is inevitable, except that the old high womanly standard of moral excellence may be no whit lowered, but may simply be carried into the wider sphere of thought and action ?

It may do much, indeed, for us that we have had such a pioneer as Harriet Martineau. It is not only that she lived so that all worthy people, however differ-

ing from her in opinion, respected and honoured her—
though that is much. It is not only that she has
settled, once for all, that a woman can be a political
thinker and a teacher from whom men may gladly
receive guidance—though that is much. But the
great value of her life to us is as a splendid example
of the moral qualities which we should carry into our
widest sphere, and which we should display in our
public exertions.

She cared for nothing before the truth; her efforts
to discover it were earnest and sincere, for she spared
no pains in study and no labour in thought in the
attempt to form her opinions correctly. Having found
what she must believe to be a right cause to uphold,
or a true word to speak, no selfish consideration intruded between her and her duty. She could risk
fame, and position, and means of livelihood, when necessary, to unselfishly support and promulgate what she
believed it to be important for mankind to do and
believe. She longed for the well-being of her kind;
and so unaffectedly and honestly that men who came
under her influence were stimulated and encouraged
by her to share and avow similar high aims. Withal,
those who lived with her loved her; she was a kind
mistress, a good friend, and tender to little children;
she was truly helpful to the poor at her gates, and her
life was spotlessly pure.

Is not this what we should all strive to be? Shall
we not love knowledge, and use it to find out truth;
and place outspoken fidelity to conscience foremost
amongst our duties; and care for the progress of our
race rather than for our own fame; shall we not be
truthful, and honest, and upright—and, to this end,
brave—in public as in private life; and shall we not

seek so to bear ourselves that men shall shrink from owning their ignobler thoughts and baser shifts to us, but shall never fear to avow high aims and pure deeds, while yet we retain our womanly kindness and all our domestic virtues unchanged?　All this we may know that we can be and do, if we will; for we have seen it exemplified in the life of Harriet Martineau.